GW01606863

The Goldmaker's House

THE GOLDMAKER'S HOUSE

by

Irmelin Sandman Lilius

translated by

Joan Tate

and illustrated by

Ionicus

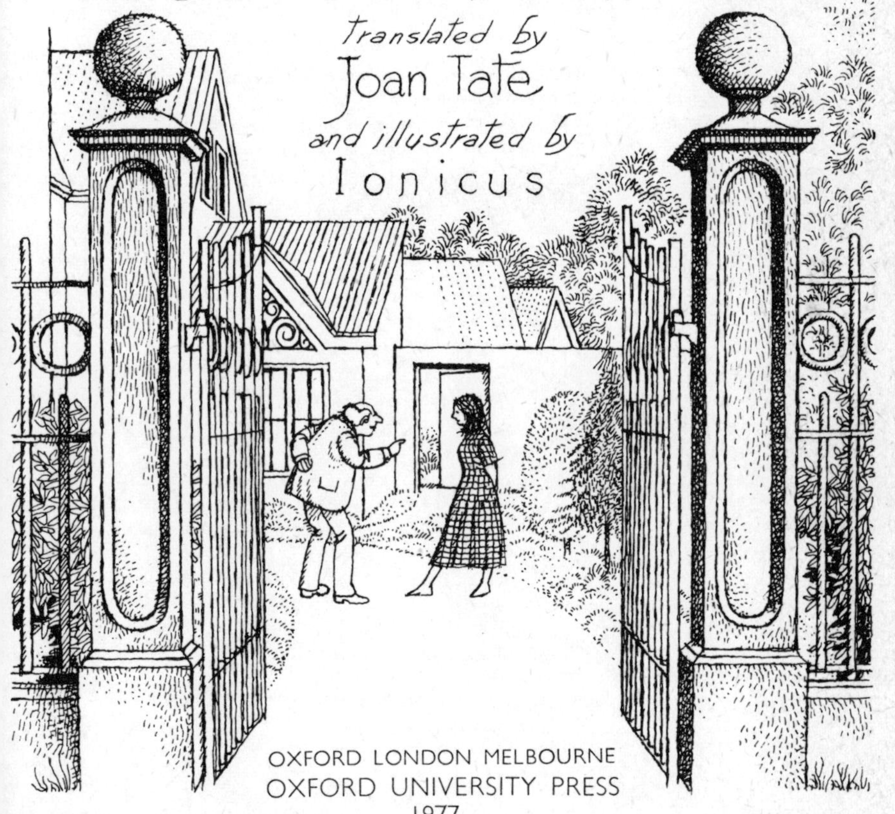

OXFORD LONDON MELBOURNE
OXFORD UNIVERSITY PRESS
1977

Oxford University Press, Walton Street, Oxford OX2 6DP

OXFORD LONDON GLASGOW
NEW YORK TORONTO MELBOURNE WELLINGTON
CAPE TOWN IBADAN NAIROBI DAR ES SALAAM LUSAKA
KUALA LUMPUR SINGAPORE JAKARTA HONG KONG TOKYO
DELHI BOMBAY CALCUTTA MADRAS KARACHI

First published by Albert Bonniers Förlag AB, Stockholm 1970
Original title: Gripanderska gården
First English edition – Oxford University Press 1977

ISBN 0 19 271401 5

Photoset by William Clowes & Sons Ltd,
The Benham Press, Colchester, Essex
and printed in Great Britain by
William Clowes & Sons Ltd,
London, Beccles & Colchester

To the memory of Marianne Helweg

Contents

ONE
The Wind

Two small streams flowed through the town of Tulavall, the Tisla and the Surbrunn, the first to the east and the second to the west. The water in both was plentiful and good, but the children considered the Tisla the more important, because it was better to play in. It rose in a crevice up on Beacon Hill and wriggled through the part of the town called Dancing End, crossed a corner of the old churchyard, curved round in a bend below and disappeared into old Gripander House garden. Then it appeared again in Market Square and followed River Sprite Lane out to the river. Where it crossed the streets, there were wooden bridges.

On one of the first really warm spring days, Bonadea and Silja Halter were paddling down at the bend of the stream below Church Slope. They were sailing bark-boats, and the most important ones were called the *Pike,* the *Emmanuel* and the *Flying Swan.* The girls were wet to their waists, but that did not matter. The south-easterly wind was blowing – the Russian Wind, as they called it around Tulavall – and the wind, so painfully icy-cold in the winter, was full of warmth and scents in the summer, making you feel airy and exhilarated, making you want to leap and jump about and breathe deeply.

Bonadea picked fresh green leaves from the limes and threaded them on to the *Emmanuel*'s masts as sails. Silja tried to man the *Pike* with ants, but they were so unskilful that she had to put them ashore again and content herself with an invisible crew. Her long fair plaits dipped into the stream as she leant forward, and then when she flung them back, they soaked her dress, so that her back was wet as well.

All the time the birds were twittering above them in as many calls as the trees had leaves and glints of light in the foliage, the scent of the balsa poplars in the Gripander garden sweeping round them. They loaded their boats with maple flowers that shone so much with honey, they had to lick them. Then they launched the boats just below the waterfall and let them race each other round the curve of the bend. If they were caught in whirlpools, they had to be poked free with a stick. Then it was a matter of catching them before the stream carried them away into the Gripander garden.

In the old days, the Gripander family had been large and wealthy (related to the aristocratic Grip family, they said, but other people said they only came from the upcountry village of Gripans). They had been merchants and brewers and had grown more powerful with each generation. They had bought the site between Market Square and Church Slope, and on the old stone foundations that had been there since time immemorial, they had built their house and brewery and warehouse – in the good times there had been a great rolling of barrels and bustling life there. But misfortune had come to both them and to the town of Tulavall. That was in the days of the dispersal and devastation of the Crimean War, with Cossacks in the hills and Englishmen at sea. People fled like straws in the wind, the Gripanders too, and when they came back, large parts of the town had been destroyed by fire.

The Gripanders had at least rescued their pride from the ruins of their greatness. They cleared their site, and on the blackened stone foundations they built another house. They built a villa of several storeys, as newfangled as possible with nooks and crannies and balconies and carvings. They painted it white and roofed it with sheet-metal. They laid out the garden in a foreign way, with plants from all over the world. They had balsa poplars and silver spruce and larch trees there, and wrought-iron fences all round. When it was all finished, something went wrong – there was no money left, several members of the family died and the survivors had to move away.

Silja's mother, who cleaned up at the mansion, used to say they were poorer than they let on. In secret, they used to mix beetroot juice with water and drink it from crystal glasses, pretending it was wine.

But people still called it 'Old Gripander House', although it had been let at second and third hand. At present, a foreign stranger whom no one knew lived there, and everyone was in some way afraid of him. Herr Turiam, he was called, whether that were his name or not, and he had not been living in the town for long before strange rumours began to go round about him: he was a sorcerer, some people said; he came from the underworld, others said; he dabbled in unholy things, and he had the town councillors utterly in his power. He had a few servants. A manservant as big as a horse and as strong as a horse – and as silent as a horse – and a housekeeper who was much the same.

'Have you ever seen that Herr Turiam?' Bonadea asked Silja, as they waded round, drops of water glittering from their fingers, their hair in their eyes and a wealth of singular goods in their ships. The three-master *Pike* under the command of Captain Halter had just tied up at Great Rock quay.

'Yes, one evening on the bridge,' said Silja. 'It was peculiar. He was rather small and looked quite ordinary, sort of thin and bent, but his eyes were horrible, truly burning under his brow. They quivered and sparked and I felt kind of peculiar all over when he looked at me . . . but then he let his eyelids fall again, and walked on. And not until he'd gone did I notice that I'd stopped when he'd fixed his eyes on me like that. Do you think it's true what they say, that he can turn the wind?'

'No,' said Bonadea, laughing, 'I don't think anyone can do that.'

As they were talking, the *Flying Swan* drifted along the stream and this time did not fasten in the backwater whirlpool as it had always done before, but sailed straight down under the fence and vanished into the Gripander garden.

'Now he's taken your boat!' said Silja. She sounded frightened.

'No, he hasn't. That was the stream,' said Bonadea. 'Come on, we'll run round and catch it as it floats out again.' She tossed her hair out of her eyes and ran down along Green Street. Silja picked up the *Pike* and the *Emmanuel* and ran after her.

There was a hawthorn hedge right round the garden inside the iron fence, unkempt and thick, impossible to see through and full of chattering sparrows. But nearest the house, facing Clapper Street, there was a timbered fence and a wooden gate. The girls lay face down where the stream ran out again. They leant over and stretched so far out that their cheeks touched the water. But the hawthorn branches grew right down over the water in an arch, and everything the stream brought with it got lodged in it. There were some of last year's dead leaves there and some dead grass and dry branches. Bonadea found a stick and poked about as far as she could reach, but she was in such an awkward position her arms got scratched, and all she could loosen was a few brown leaves.

'You'll have to make a new *Flying Swan*,' said Silja.

Bonadea raised her pointed chin and said: 'I can't make a new one, because Black Sea Sailor gave me it. I'm going to knock on the door and ask if I can fetch my boat.'

Silja shivered, but whatever she said simply made Bonadea turn more and more obstinate. With sun in her brown hair and in her red-checked dress and summer-bare feet, she marched up the steps of Gripander House and yanked at the bell-pull, Silja padding behind her, trembling but inquisitive, the *Pike* and the *Emmanuel* clutched in her wet hands.

They had to wait on the steps for a long time. Bonadea grew impatient and pulled the bell a second time – they could hear it ringing faintly and distantly far inside the house. Then the door opened and Herr Turiam was standing before them. He did not blink in the sun. His expression was neither evil nor good. He was just looking at them.

As Silja had said, there was nothing particularly remarkable about his appearance. He was thin and old and pale and wrinkled. His nose was curved and his face hollow. His white hair fluffed out round his ears and hung in a fringe over his collar. But it seemed as if the air around him was quivering – as it does in the heat of the summer above rocks, or above a fire.

And his eyes beneath the thick bushy eyebrows were sharp.

'Please may I fetch my bark-boat from the stream?' said Bonadea. But he took no notice of what she had said. He took her by the hand, and as he did so, she felt shivers run all the way up her arm. He held firmly on to her fingers, stroking her wrist with the other hand. And suddenly he gripped hard on the place where the veins run under the skin. His hands were cold, and sparkling shudders seemed to come from them.

'Yes, strong hands,' he mumbled. 'You might do.'

'Do?' said Bonadea. She was used to all kinds of people

asking her to do all kinds of things, running hither and thither on errands, helping, but she had not expected that of Herr Turiam. 'I only want my boat,' she said, and she sounded extremely timid.

'Yes, yes. You'll get your boat back,' said Herr Turiam slowly, a humming undertone like an organ in his voice. He blew on her hand. Then he looked her straight in the eyes and her heart began to thump. For his eyes were chasms with a red glow in their depths. His eyes were desolate plains beneath the setting sun. His eyes were the darkness of the universe.

'Goodbye,' she exclaimed, as she tried to jerk herself free.

But he held on even harder and said: 'Have you come only to say goodbye? Have you come only to run away again? No, you'll probably be a better assistant than anyone else in town. I didn't put that notice up just for fun.'

Then Bonadea and Silja, who was still standing trembling behind her, saw a large notice on the wall of Gripander House.

SITUATION FOR SERVANT-GIRL
APPLICATION IN PERSON
FAVOURABLE CONDITIONS

Bonadea felt caught in a noose and jumped back so quickly that Herr Turiam was jerked forward on to the top of the steps and let go her hand.

She backed away across the cobbled square.

Then Herr Turiam whistled unexpectedly shrilly, and the timbered gate was flung open by his manservant. Herr Turiam spoke to him in a foreign language, pointing, and the manservant began lumbering towards Bonadea. She turned on her heel and ran. Behind her she heard another whistle, shriller than the first, so sharp that it seemed to slice half her head off from one ear to the other ... for a moment the wind held its breath, then vanished – then it came back in a headlong rush, and now it was coming from the west, rushing in like a waterfall, so that her dress swirled round her body.

The square was not very big. She had run across it innumerable times, in all weathers, at all times of the year. But now it seemed to her to have been transformed and was stretching ahead into eternity, turning grey in the mist that was sweeping in in wave after wave. The headwind was so strong that she stumbled, feeling as if she were running uphill. Through the roar of the wind, she heard shouts and voices and glimpsed people and faces she knew. But when she stretched out her arms to them to help her – she was too out of breath to speak – they turned away. Herr Turiam's manservant was pounding closer and closer, and she could feel him panting down her neck.

Then someone else came running along with great strides and long before he had reached her and swept her up on the run without stopping, she knew who it was: the seaman stranger who was her friend. He told people his name was Jöns, but she had her own name for him, and that was Black Sea Sailor. She had not seen him for a long time. Holding her in his arms, he leapt down the slope and landed smoothly in River Street below.

The mist was so thick that they could barely see an armslength ahead of them. Bonadea was out of breath, her chest burning when she tried to speak, but Black Sea Sailor silenced her. She was sitting on his arm as if on a branch of a tree. Although she knew every corner of the town so well, she could not follow the way they were taking. She heard the manservant bellowing angrily behind them, but the sound grew fainter and finally faded away.

All this time, darkness and a penetrating glow swirled before Bonadea's eyes, refusing to go away when she closed her eyes. Nor would it go away when she blinked. Nor would it go away when she cried.

The brown water of the river was gurgling against the shore. They walked along a quay, then came to cliffs that rose higher and higher. Black Sea Sailor tramped on through grey clouds, feeling his way with his feet. Then they were bearing downhill again and she felt giddy. But he was walking with firm strides and stopped at a small ledge. The hill was smooth and brown, still warm from the sun there, though the mist made Bonadea's legs and arms shiver, and her teeth chatter as she held on to him. 'Where are we?'

'Don't you recognize it?' he said. 'On the far point of Queen's Hill, a good place to be if you want to be left in peace. Sit down, now. Put your foot in the sea, and I'll wash it for you,' he said, and only then did she notice that she had cut herself. Her big toe was bleeding from a wound as wide as a frog's mouth, the kind of wound that has a kind of lid.

There on the sea side of Queen's Hill the water was green and clear. Small conical waves pattered up, and the mist rose like mould out of them. She thrust her foot over the edge of the ledge and Black Sea Sailor washed away the congealed mass of blood and sand. Then he hauled off his 'wolf' – a big jersey was called a 'wolf' around Tulavall – and pulled it over her head. She had been allowed to borrow it before, and there must have been something special about it, because she was always warm and brave when she was wearing it.

They sat close together, their backs to the warm hill. They had a great deal to talk about, as they had not seen each other for several weeks. The mist was so thick that 'wolf' and hair and beard silvered over as they sat there.

'I've been out in the islands,' he said. 'On Silmar Island. A widower called Fridberg lives there. He owns nothing but a cabin and a boat, but he has no one to sail it for him because his sons were drowned and he can't afford to hire people. So we've come to an agreement that I sail with him and have a share in the boat as my wages – a few timbers for each trip, stumps of rope here and there. We're loading sand now and sail again early tomorrow morning.'

'I wondered where you'd been. It's been rather empty without you,' said Bonadea.

'I went off in such a hurry, there was no time to tell you,' he said. When he saw that she was still tearful, he stroked her hair and cheek, his hands rough with callouses. 'I've got sea-scorpion hands nowadays,' he said, holding them up.

'Which end of the boat have you begun on? And what's she called?' said Bonadea.

'The *Fina*. And I began in the bow, of course.'

'On the *Flying Swan* that the stream took, you were captain I was crew,' she said.

He smelt of fish and tar. His slanting greenish-blue eyes were darker than usual. There was a tense seriousness about him that she had seen only once before. That was the time when the great horses of the sea had appeared after the storm, when he had tied them up and she had been certain who he was. 'It was the whirlpools,' she said now, trying to explain. 'It was the whirlpools, and the current was stronger than I'd thought.'

'Yes, that's what it was,' he said. 'The stream can't change its course and what is undone comes closer and closer, and early tomorrow morning I must go to sea again, little *tippa*, and the time is not yet ripe.'

'Ripe? What for?' she said.

'For us to see our destiny,' he said, and he was smiling as he stroked her cheek with his forefinger. 'Where shall we end up, little *tippa*? On cold and salty rock, out on the great ocean, or shall we find ourselves a coast where the wild thyme grows, and hallow it with flaming beacons?

He talked strangely like that to her, laughing, and when her eyes stopped smarting, he said: 'Do what you have to do. As long as your heart burns like a sun, darkness can do nothing to you.'

She came wandering through the streets early next morning. She had spent the night on board the *Fina* and waved her off at dawn as she sailed away with old Fridberg and Black Sea Sailor on board. The air was cool and damp, but the mist had gone. She was limping a little, but smiling to herself, and she was still wearing the 'wolf'. But then she heard voices behind a fence: 'What was all that fuss yesterday?'

'Didn't you hear? Two street brats were creating havoc at Gripander House – yes, one of them was that Bonadea they had so much trouble with at the orphanage – well, they kept ringing the doorbell and running away, the wicked things, at least that's what I heard – and in the end Herr Turiam got tired of it and caught one of them . . . what? Yes, the other one ran off and the mist came down so suddenly, she got away, but no doubt they'll be in trouble for causing all that . . . '

As Bonadea went on, she was no longer smiling. She turned off the Esplanade, rounded the Town Hall corner and walked slowly up across the Square. She caught a glimpse of Silja's mother over in the shadow of the trees of West Wood. As she walked as straight as an arrow across the cobbles that still had shadowy arches of dew along their backs, she thought that she had been heading this way all her life. She had always managed to get away in twists and turns, and she had swung herself free to left and right – many a time. Many, many times. Many. But now an end had come to that game. Now she had to go to the end of the road.

And not stop to think. And not let fear take hold. She did not feel her bad foot, but just walked and walked, step by step like a ticking clock, across the square and up the steps of Gripander House. When she reached the top step, the door opened slightly. Silja slithered out and stood there with her back to the wall, her eyes red, her dress crumpled, and she was still clutching her bark-boats.

Bonadea saw all this out of the corner of her eye as she took the last steps in the sun, but just as the door closed behind her, she thought: 'I managed to get Silja out, so part of me got away this time, too.'

TWO
The Illness

Silja was walking home with her mother and the wind was warm. The road was uphill all the way, and mamma walked more and more slowly, almost as if her knees were giving way. Up on Crooked Hill, near Gold Crown corner where they lived, they met a man Silja did not know. He was rather short and squat, with a ring in one ear and tattooing on his hands. He came straight up to them and said to mamma: 'How are things, Emmeline?'

She stopped and straightened up, just on the line between sunlight and shadow. 'All right,' she said in a faint voice.

Then he took her hand and raised it to him, saying in a low and insistent voice: 'Emmeline . . .'

Silja watched mamma looking fixedly at the man's face, then gazing far away into the sky, her face dulled and expressionless from fatigue. 'I can't,' she said, and the man dropped her hand. She walked on without looking back, as heavily as if walking in a marsh.

'Mamma, who was that?' said Silja, when they had gone up the hill a bit. When she glanced back, she saw that he was still standing there, his arms hanging.

'Someone I got to know down at the harbour,' she replied.

'Why did he call you Emmeline? When your name's Emma?'

Mamma was silent for a moment, and then she said vehemently: 'I've always thought Emma sounds like mamma . . . like some kind of thing, not the name of a person. Emmeline is nicer.'

Silja said nothing to that, but her forehead creased with her thoughts. After a while, she understood. In the stories pappa told them, there were often three princesses: Merula, Mira and Marinina, so without saying much about it, Sanna, Silja and Sissela had each taken on themselves one princess. But pappa had never said a word about a queen with a royal name that might suit mamma Emma.

They turned into Bulder's at the corner of Gold Crown Street and Gold Crown Lane, where it was green with knot-grass and camomile at this time of year and the lilac round the outhouses was in flower. Lussa, their cat, was sitting in the sun, licking her paw.

In the porch, they were met with smoke and a great deal of coughing. 'Is that you, mamma?' said Sanna, when they went in. 'I thought I'd have the coffee ready when you got back, but the stove just keeps on smoking . . .'

'You should have closed the doors and windows properly before you started, then there's no cross-draught,' said mamma. She got down on her knees by the stove and riddled and raked, which helped almost immediately. The flames rose like yellow ribbons.

'Smoke's coming out of the chimney now,' cried Sissela from outside.

When the air in the kitchen had cleared a little, they saw that Mother Blomfors, their immediate next-door neighbour, was there. 'I came in to borrow some sugar,' she said, holding out a mug and laughing. 'I couldn't get the stove going, either, although I offered. But your love is strong, Emma.'

Mamma stared at her.

'That's what they say if you've got a good hand with fire,' said Mother Blomfors.

'I have five children,' said mamma slowly.

Silja wanted to cry out: 'No, you've got four . . . us three girls and Stefan at sea.' But then she realised that mamma had meant that pappa was also like a child, sitting there in the

bedroom with a hole in his head, unable to do anything except make nets and tell stories.

Mother Blomfors' voice sounded quite different when she answered.

'Yes, it's a heavy burden you have to bear. You have to find solace where you can, I can see that. No one would think ill of you for that.'

'You're mistaken,' said mamma, in a voice so cutting, bitter and hopeless that no one could answer. She tipped some sugar lumps into Mother Blomfors' mug and Mother Blomfors patted her thin shoulder in thanks, then left without another word.

That was the moment when mamma fell ill. Grey in the face, she sat at the table without drinking her coffee. When Sanna asked if they could have a little butter today, she did not reply. The girls looked at each other anxiously, but before they had time to do anything, she fell off the chair, almost flowing off it on to the floor.

They leapt up so that the chairs scraped loudly. Sissela began to cry, Sanna fetched water in the scoop and Silja ran for help. She had only thought of going to ask Mother Blomfors to come, but fat Aunt Lingon in the house across the yard happened to be waddling past, as well as the little Walloon lacemaker, on her way to the market with her basket on her arm. Very soon there was quite a crowd round the steps into the Halters' house. Old Man Bulder came spitting round the corner and cried out in his high tremulous voice: 'She's not too ill to pay the rent, is she?' But Mother Blomfors had left her brood of breakfast-eaters for Beata, her eldest daughter, to look after. She forged her way through the crowd like a snowplough and it was she and her small husband who lifted Mother Halter up from the floor and put her to bed.

Sanna had bathed her forehead with water so that there was a whole pool on the floor, and as Emma's coffee was untouched and it seemed a pity to waste it, Mother Blomfors picked up the cup and drained it. She knew that Doctor Skrållberg was away, and the strange doctor who had come in his place was no great joy to anyone. So it would be best to summon Klockarback-Fia. You did not have to pay her until you could.

It could be said that the girls were a little frightened of Klockarback-Fia. She was very old and small and hunch-backed, brown in the face all the year round, and she sold herbs and vegetables and medicinal plants in the market. She could cure all kinds of illnesses, invisible and visible, and she had powers others did not possess – there were strange rumours about her. But Bonadea was a friend of hers. Anyhow, at the moment mamma's illness was a greater terror. Sanna went to find her.

When she came back bringing Fia with her, mamma was awake, but very weak and pale round the mouth. She had asked Silja to wash her with a flannel, undo her plait and comb her hair neatly. Silja knelt down and combed as gently as she could. If she pulled even slightly, mamma groaned. She said her head felt tender, her whole body felt tender, and even the sheets hurt. Pappa sat in his usual corner, looking at her with his eyes wide open, without moving or saying anything.

Klockarback-Fia, crumpled and dry as an old leaf, but with eyes as clear as water, leant over and pressed her middle finger against mamma's forehead at the top of her nose. 'I've cured you before,' she said as she took her hand away.

'That you haven't,' Sanna dared protest.

Klockarback-Fia turned to her and laughed quietly. 'When you're as old as I am, you muddle people up but not their destinies,' she said.

'I'm, sinking,' gasped mamma, trying to sit up. Fia pressed her gently down again, and with her hands on her shoulders, said: 'We'll sail a long way still. I'll cure you if you promise to trust me completely.'

Then mamma nodded and calmed down and lay still.

'I'll come with a cart for her as soon as I can,' said Fia. 'Protect her from evil tongues and keep her warm. But open the window on to the street.'

'Where are you going to take her?' said Sanna.

'Out to my place at Klockarbacken, where she'll have wild strawberries and goat's milk and green leaves,' said Fia.

When she had gone, Sanna said: 'She's *muddly* in the head. She talks such nonsense. But I suppose she'll have to take mamma as mamma wants to go. And how do we protect her from evil tongues?'

'We mustn't let anyone in,' said Silja.

In the daytime it was not so noticeable that mamma had gone. She was so often somewhere else anyhow – she went out cleaning and washing and so on, here and there at the gentry's houses in the town. But the evenings were empty.

The girls used to lay the table and put the potato pan on the stove, and then at about six o'clock they would keep a lookout for her and run to meet her when she came into the street, helping her carry if her basket were heavy. Sometimes she might have funny things with her from the houses she cleaned. Sometimes they were old books – like *Bird Hans* or *Reading for*

Children – sometimes it might be odd cups and saucers of real porcelain, only a little cracked. Once that spring it had been a parcel of old clothes Countess Kattstedt had given her with the words: 'I'm sure you can alter them for your children.' Mamma had smiled wryly when the parcel was undone, and the children squealed with delight. They were mostly old-fashioned outworn ball-dresses. There was a crinoline of emerald-green silk, as wide as a circus tent, but so narrow at the waist that Sissela was the only one who could get into it. There was another of blue velvet with a squared pattern in darkened gold, as splendid as a summer sea, but so fragile that you could see straight through it. And there was also a strange costume of lilac chiffon, probably a fancy-dress costume, mamma said. It was as narrow as a tube and difficult to get into, but covered with diagonal frills and flounces and trains. The girls at once dressed up and ran out into the yard, the flounces dragging behind them, stumbling and fooling about and talking grandly. There was also the bodice of a black dress with puffed sleeves as large as beer-kegs and fringes of jet beads, and one single item that mamma could make into something, a curtain of green wool, only slightly moth-eaten. She thought she would make winter dresses from it for Sanna and Silja. But the girls didn't like it, because the material was coarse and itchy.

Sanna and Silja and Sissela shared out the household chores as best they could. Sissela did the cooking and Silja the cleaning. Sanna had found work on her own accord at the pottery down by the river, and she took command. Sissela maintained that *washing* the potatoes was part of cleaning, so Silja should do that, and there was a good deal of bickering over it. But gradually they got used to it all. Every time Stefan came home from a fishing trip, he brought a box of buckling, the small smoked herrings they loved. So they lived well then and could exchange some of them for milk. Then they made rhubarb fool. Out at the back up towards the hill was a whole wild forest of rhubarb that anyone from the yards could take. And they made nettle soup with segments of egg in it, because Bonadea's black hen, Cacklehilda, had quite unexpectedly come flying in and had settled down with them. At first, the girls were afraid Lussa would eat her, but at their very first encounter Cacklehilda had pecked so fiercely at Lussa, that Lussa decided on her part that she would pretend Cacklehilda was simply not there.

But a number of questions arose with the hen. Where was Bonadea these days? If she had gone away for a while, for she did have friends here and there, then why hadn't she told them beforehand and said goodbye? People often asked after her.

The only two people who knew where she was were Mother Halter, who had waited all night in West Wood, unable to emerge, unable to go home, and Silja. But mamma was ill at Fia's and Silja could not possibly bring herself to tell what she knew. The very thought of Bonadea hurt her chest and made her eyes smart. She remembered Aunt Lingon's stories about girls being spirited away and having their minds perverted, and when she sneaked round Gripander House, it seemed to her as high and brooding as a mountain.

She crept right round Gripander House trying to see through iron railings and leafy undergrowth. She climbed the limes by Church Slope and tried to see in from there. She lay down in the dust of the street and peered under the wooden gate. And faintly and miserably, she tried to whistle the songs Bonadea used to hum about 'the deer with her brown hair'. Once she got a reply and was really frightened.

She dreamed at night they were sailing in the Tisla and it was wider than in reality. Bonadea was a little brown bark-boat dancing along the stream. Then she glided under the fence, and although Silja hurled herself forward, she could not catch it. She felt it slipping through her fingers and being sucked away into the whirlpools.

Early one morning, she went down to the bend in the stream by Church Slope. She had loaded the *Pike* and the *Emmanuel* with drops of cherry resin that were hard and yellowish-brown like amber, and with a tiny sliver of porcelain with a very beautiful rose on it, and with a mother-of-pearl button and a few peppercorns. She launched them carefully and let them sail away into the Gripander garden.

THREE
The Fire

Never had Bonadea lived through such long drawn-out days as those first four or five at Gripander House. She saw nothing of Herr Turiam. The housekeeper was forbidding and taciturn, only snorting whenever Bonadea asked a question. Jakem, the manservant, was foreign and did not speak at all.

Bonadea had to sweep and clean in the big house, where it was all so quiet that a crackle in the wall or a creak of a board made her jump. The housekeeper led her from room to room, her hand fiercely gripping her arm, and she locked the doors all round her. She was not allowed at all into some of the rooms. When she defiantly said you don't need to pinch me so hard, all you have to do is tell me where I mustn't go, the housekeeper just said contemptuously: 'You can never trust people like you,' and set her to polishing copper, scouring knives and mending ragged curtains in a room that had obviously never been inhabited.

But Bonadea could not believe they had urged and insisted that she come to this house just to do all these little jobs. She could not believe otherwise than that her real task lay ahead of her. And waiting quietly in ignorance she had always found difficult.

She was given a little room to herself in a projection high up under the roof, in the corner facing Market Square and Green Street, with a balcony, a glass pane in the balcony door and two small round eyes for windows. She always sat there when the housekeeper was not keeping her busy. She watched people coming and going. She heard horses clattering past, wheels and cabriolets rattling, the ladies of the town riding along beneath parasols and shady hats, rocking in time and out, talking together. The plasterer came swearing along with his bony old horse, Bearmeat, pulling much too heavy a load. Alderman Pilot came driving his Trotter – and young Count Ärenport rode his new thoroughbred Bernina that looked like brown silk all over.

She saw all three of the Halter girls going to Klockarback-Fia's stall in the square and she wondered what they were talking about for so long. She also saw Silja prowling around alone when evening came, drooping and anxious, but determined. Then she stuck out her head and whistled faintly, pointing with her thumb at the front door, for she thought they might be able to talk through the letter-box.

She opened the door into the corridor, where a late shaft of sunlight was floating through the gable window, and she crept along the dusty shaft. But the boards creaked, and anxiety made her twice as heavy as usual on the stairs. But she got down to the hall, and there she could see Silja like a shadow against the opaque glass in the door. 'I'm here,' she said, her mouth against the letter-box, and Silja's slim fingers poked the flap up from outside.

'How're things with you? Are they nasty to you?'

'No. It's all right. Though it's hard work,' Bonadea whispered back. 'Look after Cacklehilda for me, will you? I don't know how long this might go on for.'

At that moment she felt a hard grip on her arm, a grip that numbed her whole arm, and the housekeeper was there, her face harsh.

'Didn't I tell you,' she hissed. '*Untrustworthy . . .*'

Bonadea clenched her teeth. The flap of the letter-box snapped shut. Then she saw Silja press her thumb against the glass so that it showed as a little white spot. Bonadea immediately put her thumb against it and felt the glass grow warm. The housekeeper jerked her roughly away from the door, away from the hall, but as she was dragged through the doorway into the kitchen corridor, she could still see Silja's thumb like a little white moon in the yellowish-grey glass of the door.

After that, she dared not let her presence be known when she saw Silja prowling round the house. And she was generally careful not to be seen out – neither called to nor questioned and be forced to admit that she was caught.

But when the Russian wind blew, she felt her whole soul flying, lifting in the headwind like a bird and being carried away to the long free shores to the east of the town. She felt it in her bones that if only she were free to run there, she would experience something wonderful. She heard the gulls screaming and her very longing pained her.

The garden at Old Gripander House covered a large piece of the unevenly sloping hill. There were trees there from the time of the very first Gripanders, scarred by fire but still green, as well as ruins of the brewery and mossy walls that were even older. Bushes and undergrowth and a wealth of plants had all grown tangled together. There were plenty of birds, as well as hedgehogs and other small creatures. Bonadea was allowed out in it one day. The housekeeper opened the door and pointed.

'That's the carrot bed. Weed it and thin them. Come in when it's done.'

Bonadea crouched down over the carrot bed, and the scent of the soil immediately below her nose was so strong that tears came into her eyes and she had to laugh. The earth smells, titt tott, Bonadea. All's well with the world, here's a juicy stalk and here's an earthworm. She worked until the tips of her fingers turned green and her nails were black with earth. She found a rusty nail and a sliver of glass and several pieces of bone, and she thought about all kinds of things, and about what she had heard tell of Countess Morrstjärna: every morning the Countess stepped out into her garden and said: 'Good-morning, carrots.' And then the carrots bowed in the dust and replied: 'Good-morning, Your Ladyship.'

The sun was hot on the back of her neck, her shadow like a trailing apron. A few steps away from her, another

shadow floated out across the carrot bed. It was Herr Turiam's. She had not noticed him coming. But when she saw his shadow, she stopped weeding and sat back on her heels. She looked at him and did not know what to say.

He was also silent for a long time before he said: 'Are you afraid of me today, too?'

Bonadea did not know why, but in this flood of sunlight, the scent of the earth and leaves, with a blackbird singing halfway between her head and the sky, Herr Turiam seemed less important than a worm. 'No,' she said.

He nodded and asked another question. 'Why were you

afraid the first time?'

'Because you frightened me, of course. And why did you take Silja?'

'So that you would come back again. Well, if you hadn't, we would have let her go, of course, because she was no good at all, far too timid. And her mother kept calling her with such disturbing persistence. Yes, her mother must have a very strong soul, although she looks so frail. But if you'd not come back, that would only have meant that you were no good, either. It's difficult to get helpers these days.'

Bonadea stared at him and said nothing, trying to make out what he meant. Then she said: 'You promised I could have my bark-boat back.'

'Take it,' he said.

She searched along the Tisla. The stream looped its way through the garden, forming pools with banks of brown leaves round the edges, and rustling waterfalls. In many places the undergrowth was so thick that she had to bend double as she waded, had hands on her head to prevent her hair getting caught. Then she came to a sunny terrace, where there were water-lilies and irises in a pond, and pondweed. Herr Turiam was standing on the mossy stones at the edge, waiting for her. The *Flying Swan* lay in the pondweed, her sails withered.

The blackbird sang in the tall balsa poplar. Bonadea looked up and felt like the blackbird herself. A gull swept over them, and she felt as strong as a gull. She felt like a ladybird. 'I've always wanted to know what it looked like here!' she said.

He looked pleased and asked her to look around.

On the other side of the pool was a derelict summer house consisting of nothing but pillars with twisting honeysuckle winding up them, and a conical roof. Herr Turiam was sitting there with his eyes closed. When Bonadea had run round the garden, she stopped in front of him and looked at him. He was like an old tree. He was like one of those wooden saints in church, when the paint has long since flaked off, but that didn't matter because then you saw the shape much better. His nose was curved in a sweeping line, his high cheekbones and high forehead making him look for *one* moment, one moment only, like Black Sea Sailor. He looked worn, weather-beaten and weather-torn, indefatigably tough.

Suddenly he opened his dark eyes and turned them on her so abruptly that she jumped, and he said: 'What are you thinking about?'

She answered honestly.

'About whether it's true that you're a sorcerer.'

'Is that what people say about me?'

'They say all sorts of things.'

'What do they say?'

She hesitated, but then obediently repeated everything she had heard; that he was considered to be a sorcerer and that he brooded over his treasure and that he was a maker of gold.

'In some ways,' said Herr Turiam slowly, 'all that is true. I am an alchemist, and alchemy has not a very good reputation in our time. But it is a noble old science, full of secrets. Alchemy is the science of Transformation and Renewal of Matter – yes, you could say it is related to sorcery, and also to astronomy and mathematics, to poetry and the knowledge of plants. As far as gold is concerned, I have not yet been able to achieve any – so far. And it's beginning to be rather necessary for me to make some.'

He smiled slightly at Bonadea's impressed expression and explained quite simply: 'Research work of that kind is expensive. I've spent all the money I've ever had and now live off loans – I've pawned my vision and my perseverance, as well as my whole destiny.'

The blackbird sang above their heads and its notes poured down like a brilliant shaft of light through the leaves. 'Do you

know anything about sorcery?' said Herr Turiam abruptly.

Bonadea tried to remember what Klockarback-Fia had once said, that 'real sorcery is a serious matter'. Herr Turiam raised his stick and pointed at a stone on the slope. 'Try lifting that up,' he said.

The stone lay in its nest in the earth, warm towards the sun and with a cap of moss. Underneath it, a whole lot of creepy-crawlies hurriedly scuttled away when she grasped it and hauled it out, her arm muscles tensed. The stone was as large as a porridge pan. She panted and shifted it laboriously towards her knees.

'Put it down again now,' said Herr Turiam, and she did so.

But when she let it go and rubbed her sore hands together, the stone slowly tipped out of its hole again, turning its damp belly upwards and rolling down the slope. Grass and flowers were flattened and rose again as it passed. It rolled over to the pool, curled itself round on the uneven edge of the pool, hesitated, collected itself and glided out from the edge. It was floating like a bark-boat, ripples trembling all round it.

Then Herr Turiam began to speak again, as if to crowds of listeners. Perhaps the whole garden was full of invisible people.

'They say "dead as a stone", but that is wrong,' he said. 'In all of nature, there is nothing quite without life. But the forms of life are different. What do you think about the soul?'

Again Bonadea thought about Klockarback-Fia, who had said: '... long will live he who has great longing ... lifting one above the little troubles that otherwise embitter our days,' 'Soul means Longing,' said Bonadea.

He nodded several times. 'The soul is fire. The soul is the concealed fire that burns in all things visible. It is our gift and our true heritage, but it scorches, it scorches. See, it wants to come out. And it drives one to singular activities. Sorcery,' said Herr Turiam, 'it is the drawing out from things of the power that lies inside them ... first one gets a stone rolling. Gradually, with a strong will, one can induce things to do what is essentially against their nature. One entices out the invisible fire that is the soul of things, and forces it to obedience. Mastering it.'

He was moving his right hand in broad sweeps as he spoke.

'But does it like it?' said Bonadea.

Herr Turiam smiled, a crooked, half-grim, half-bitter smile. 'Everything man does devours, devours and destroys.'

All this time, he had kept his eyes fastened on the stone, but at Bonadea's question and his own answer, it shuddered and sank, circular rings at once forming on the surface as if from an ordinarily thrown stone. Bonadea held her head in both hands – she was dizzy, trying to understand. The empty hole in the earth gaped at her, the ants that had lived there having all retreated even deeper down into the ground.

'All my life I have sought what is beyond the visible,' said Herr Turiam, looking tired now, very old and very tired. 'Knowledge and yet more knowledge. Roads that no one has trodden before. Means of cleansing and transformation, called the Stone, or the Elixir – I myself call it Arcanum, which means secret. It is so powerful that the soul rejoices even in the search. Sometimes I have thought that a few more nights' work was all that was needed. I have struggled on along endlessly long roads. But always there has been a little air between, which means that I do not get there. Ramon Lull could transform himself into a scarlet cockerel. Arnoldo di Todi found a way of going back into the past. Doctor Martinus of Åbo ended up in a lunatic asylum – the most wonderful things become possible, but an invisible road is hard to walk for us who are imprisoned, each one in his own body.'

Suddenly Bonadea understood why he had gone to so much trouble. 'You want me to help you,' she said.

'I need help from someone who is my opposite,' he said. 'For a while. A little while. And you needn't be afraid that I'll devour you, as it is precisely your strength I need.'

'Ah . . . well,' she said. 'I suppose I could try.' And although her head whirled as she said it, she thought at the same time: what else could she do? And she was full of curiosity – she wanted to see more miracles and acts of sorcery. She wanted to feel again the sweetness and strength and wonder one feels when one strains every muscle and nerve with all one's power and succeeds in something difficult, like sailing in a swinging wind. And if it was dangerous, then all of life was dangerous.

The housekeeper said nothing whatsoever when Herr Turiam told her that Bonadea need not help in the house any longer. But she made a lot of faces. If she met Bonadea in a room or in the kitchen, she turned her back on her to avoid having to see her. Bonadea ignored her and even the bruises on her arms, because now she had more important things to think about. But she finished weeding the vegetable patch all the same, and cut pea-sticks from up in the undergrowth.

FOUR
The Copper Gate

Every Tuesday and Thursday, and on Saturdays, Sanna and Silja and Sissela went down to the square where Klockarback-Fia had her little barrow. She answered their questions as to how mamma was. 'She'll get better, but it'll take time. She's still very tired.'

After a few weeks, Sanna was allowed to go back to Klockarbacken with her. When she came back home, she was looking serious. 'Mamma's probably been much worse than we thought,' she said to her sisters. 'Fia's cut her hair off, because it got so sweaty and tangled from her fever, and she's as pale as a cloven potato and can hardly move her eyes. And yet, Fia says she's much better now.'

'What did she say? Did she send any message to us?'

'She didn't say much. Oh, yes, she said that when Fia was out feeding the animals or picking herbs or at the market, there was a tiny, tiny little old woman, only about an ell high, who was otherwise exactly like Fia and who looks after her.'

Silja and Sissela gazed wide-eyed at her. 'I suppose she's still a bit delirious,' said Sanna.

'Did she say when she was coming home?'

'No . . .'

'Did she cry?'

'Yes,' said Sanna, with a sigh. 'So I told her she wasn't to worry, that we were coping very well – well, we *are*,' said Sanna sternly, although no one had even thought of contradicting her. 'And Fia gave us this side of pork. They gave it to her at Jetisbacka, for curing the rash on their mother's leg. And when I said: you can't go giving away a whole side, she just laughed and said that she was too small and withered for such a huge piece, and youngsters like us could perhaps manage it. We'll have to clean a bit better before mamma comes back, I suppose,' said Sanna, looking round.

'I *think* I sweep properly,' said Silja guiltily.

'And how's your mamma, then?' the women in the yard asked almost every day. The girls always replied: 'She's better, thank you.' Then the one who had asked tut-tutted and shook her head, saying: 'Yes, a fever of the nerves, that's no laughing matter, that isn't. So young, too. But she's been delicate for a long time . . .'

'Just as if we'd said: "She's worse, thank you!"' said Sanna crossly, glaring back at them.

The women talked about all kinds of cases of illness they knew or had heard about. Mother Kröpelin's eldest sister had also been pale and thin like that, and she had worked herself to death, she had, when her husband had been lost at sea and she had been left alone with eight children in Crowfield, where everyone had nits so that you could hardly get the comb through their hair. 'But she was much better-looking than Mother Halter, before she lost her teeth, of course,' Mother Kröpelin added, as if that were any consolation.

Sanna forced open the kitchen window facing on to Gold Crown Lane, which had been nailed up for as long as they could remember, and the girls began secretly getting in and out that way to escape meeting the women and any more of their talk that seared their minds.

'But they're kind, *too*,' said Silja, whose conscience was so easily touched. That was the day when the Walloon lacemaker had given them a toffee each, and Mother Blomfors had undertaken to do their washing. The washing was such heavy work for Silja that she just wept and rubbed her knuckles raw.

One Sunday, when Fia said they were to go out to

Klockarbacken to see mamma, they got up early. It was warm and sunny, a light breeze coming from the sea. Sanna put out sour milk for pappa in case he grew thirsty, with a saucer on top of it to keep it from filling up with flies. Sissela put out her dolls, Lottikin and Tomkin, in a row together with some wooden animals Uncle Blomfors had carved for her, so that pappa would have some company.

They washed carefully and put on clean, unironed dresses. Ironing was hot and troublesome work and you soon got crumpled, anyhow, they said sensibly to each other. They combed each other's hair and tried not to yelp when it got pulled by mistake. They each took a basket in case they found any wild strawberries. Fia had said that wild strawberries were powerful food, either you couldn't tolerate them, and then you at once became red and pimply just like a wild strawberry itself, or else you tolerated them. And as mamma was one of those who tolerated them, she should have as many as possible.

The girls jumped out through the window. Gold Crown Lane ran out into a gully up towards the hill. Yellow splashes of stonecrop shone there, and there was also a wild jungle of briar-rose and bird-cherry that was wonderful to play in. There were wild strawberry flowers there too, but no ripe berries, because the kids from the yards round about pulled them all off before they were ripe.

The girls hurried up through the gully, over Beacon Hill, and out along the east road, past Holy Irina's church and the shabby collection of houses called Crowfield. It was much worse there than at Dancing End, where they themselves lived, dirty and ugly and flat, as it had been built on a field. The girls hurried past, but no one came out and yelled at them, and none of the Crowfield dogs even barked. It was too early still.

When the girls were right out of town, they slowed down. They leapt across the ditches to the right and left, searching for wild strawberries and picking flowers. And now that no one could hear them and say 'Having such fun when your mother's so ill!' they talked and laughed about everything they saw.

They came to Lutas farm up on a hill, and Sanna pointed to the field below. 'That's where the battle was. The Battle of Lutas. We read about it at school. The enemy came marching in, three hundred men strong, and the Tulavallans went out to meet them. This was where they met and fought. Even today people plough up buttons and bullets and medals and things like that from the field. And when there's a storm or mist, they see the battle all over again, up in the air. Rudolf the poet has written a poem about it.'

Silja thought it must have been difficult to fight in a field where there were so many ditches. They should have stuck to the road instead, she said, like the boys when they played five-a-side with sticks and a puck in the evenings.

Klockarbacken lay a bit away from the main road, to the right when you came out of town. There had been a little village there once upon a time, five small farms nestling close to each other like hens on a perch. But they had burnt down. Perhaps at the same time as the Battle of Lutas, Silja said. The people living there had moved away. All that was left was a tiny cottage on the south slope, and that was Fia's.

The girls took a short cut diagonally across the meadow where Fia's old horse was grazing, and then they heard the cuckoo. So they ran after the sound to get under the tree where it was, so that they could wish. They crept as quietly as they could and he cuckooed and cuckooed, and then they came to the back of Fia's cottage, where they stopped at the sound of voices.

Mamma was lying in a hammock between two trees. Fia was sitting in the grass sorting herbs. The cuckoo called one last time, then flew off into the forest. But the girls stayed standing there, because mamma was talking and her voice did not sound as it usually did, but was grating and plaintive. She was saying: 'It's so difficult . . .'

'You've kept going from sheer willpower for many years,' said Fia. 'And your body has complied. So it's no wonder that you fell ill when your will cracked.'

'There are so many who need me,' said mamma.

Klockarback-Fia was silent for a moment, then said emphatically: 'They need someone who is alive. We have enough of the dead as it is. And you know just as well as I do that there are two ways of dying.'

Then she fell silent again for a while before saying:

'That night a little while ago, when you got so cold, then you nearly went. And I began to grieve. When you stood there at the gate . . .'

The girls heard their mother sigh, then say: 'Yes, my hands grew numb, my feet, too, and I felt the cold creeping all over me, and I thought: is this what it's like? I knew you were close by, but I didn't see you.'

'But weren't you afraid?'

'No, not in the slightest. Nor tired. And I had no pain anywhere – it was as if I were young again. It was the time before that things were difficult, when everything I liked most lost all meaning, when I noticed how I became more and more detached from my body, and everything grew severe and tall

all round me. But that night I heard music in great waves, and I very much wanted to go. There was only one single thread that held me back. Fia!' said mamma fiercely. 'The most difficult thing was to be pulled back and be burdened and weak again!'

'And yet,' said Fia. 'You were pleased to stay. As long as there's someone left on earth who wants to see us again, we're pleased to stay. I know that only too well.' She thought for a moment, and then said: 'Him, Halter, your husband, must have told you the story about the bird, hasn't he?'

'Many a time, but I can't bear listening to his stories any longer,' mamma said.

'Then I'll tell it to you now, and you must listen. Once upon a time there was a king who was transformed into a bird . . .'

The girls stood silently in the bushes. They recognized the story, and yet it sounded different from when pappa told it.

'. . . into a bird that sang beautifully. And his queen put him in a cage so that he could live in safety. She watched over him day and night. She didn't understand that he wanted to fly freely in his bird-life and accept his bird-death when it came. And she didn't understand that at the same time she was making herself a prisoner.'

The cuckoo called in the distance. The wind came in gusts.

'That feels like a knife in my heart,' said mamma.

'Few people,' said Fia, 'can live a whole long life without a knife in breast or head. But you've still got time. It'll be some time yet before you're on your feet again.'

'And what shall I live off when I can't work any longer? Advise me, Fia.'

'Wait,' said Fia. 'Decisions ripen, they mature. Don't try to pick them unripe.'

Sanna backed away, pulling the other two with her when the next gust came and drowned the rustle they made. They went a long way round up the hill and down again, arriving at Fia's cottage the usual way between the hedges of overgrown lilac. Mamma was lying there, her hair like a little cap of fur, the hammock swaying slowly.

'You look like a tiny baby, mamma,' said Sissela.

'I've a christening gown on, too,' said mamma, and her voice sounded just as usual, tired, but without that cutting tone. She turned back the woollen shawl at her throat and showed them the fine linen shift with lace round it that Fia had lent her.

The older girls did not really know what to say. Fia brought out a large bowl of clotted milk and three spoons for them, as well as bread and cheese. They sat down in the grass and ate. Mamma praised them for their harvest of wild strawberries, and Fia chatted about her medicinal plants and how they should be used: lilies of the valley for heart trouble, coltsfoot for a cough, and so on.

When they were leaving, Fia came with them for a bit down the road. Sanna said: 'We heard a little of what you were talking about . . . we couldn't help it.'

'It doesn't matter that you have ears,' said Fia. 'As long as you have wits in the place between them.'

Silja was to look after Sissela in the daytime, while Sanna was at the pottery and Stefan at sea, and the task weighed heavily on her mind. Johan Flinck the vagrant, a pleasant, kindly soul, had begun to take pappa with him out on fishing trips. He had only one arm so needed someone to row. They were often away for days. They got fresh fish from the sea and had bread and coffee with them, as well as something strong in a small bottle, Sanna suspected, but she could do nothing about that.

Once Sissela escaped from Silja and was away all day.

They had been to the market to talk to Klockarback-Fia and given her a fistful of strawberries for mamma. They had been given them by Countess Morrstjärna's gardener as wages for helping him pick out snails. And then they had bathed at the shallow Longsand beach in their grey-striped flannel drawers, because there had been boys there, too. They had met Mrs Pompilias' daughters from Vackerbacka farm up the river, and Sissela had begun to play with Peppina, the youngest of them. They were to go home for sour milk with pieces of bread in, and Silja ran ahead, because she had been in the water for so long that her teeth were chattering and her fingers white. She hung her drawers out to dry, put a bowl for each of them on to the table, praised Lussa, who came in with a wretched rat, and she had given water to Cacklehilda. But Sissela did not come. Silja ate on her own, slowly splashing with her spoon as she read *The King's Ring* that someone had lent her.

"... Bad omens!" muttered the Count between his teeth. He rushed out with fantastic zeal to place himself at the spearhead of the defence of the castle.

At this time the queen was thirty-two years old, but still retained much of the beauty of her youth.

And the silence of the night set seal to this fearful oath.

"Are you not well, my lady ..."

Gradually Silja grew cross, and then anxious. All that long hot afternoon, mortally afraid, she ran in and out of the yard that smelt of camomile and rubbish and new timber, because Blomfors was making something in his shed. As if tethered by a short rope, she ran back and forth, and each time she set off down Gold Crown Street or up Gold Crown Lane or into the gulley, she thought, of course, Sissela would come in the other direction, and when she finds I'm not at home, she'll go looking for me, and then we'll never find each other ...

In the end, she just walked between the kitchen and the bedroom, sobbing tearlessly and twisting her hands and seeing little Sissela drowned, gored, wet and blood-stained, imprisoned, lost, hungry and tired. She saw Sissela helplessly weeping.

So late that afternoon, when the slow sun had reached the lane window and the flies were thudding against the glass, and she heard Sissela singing out there, she was so relieved that her anger overwhelmed her once again. She looked out. There was Sissela slowly trudging down Gold Crown corner, singing dreamily, her clear voice floating ahead of her, her eyes on the sky and a world of her own, both hands full of drooping flowers.

And what did she have in her hair if not a hedgehog skin?

Silja leapt out of the window, landing so badly on her heels that it hurt, rushed up and grabbed hold of her to make sure that the danger was now over, and began to shake her and shout.

'Ow!' said Sissela, dropping her flowers. 'Mind my crown. My crown!' she whimpered, starting to cry, just as Silja had imagined her all afternoon. Silja was dreadfully ashamed. 'Come in and eat, anyhow,' she said more calmly, trying to take off the crown. It was made of burrs.

Sissela put her nose in the air and sniffed. 'I don't want your horrid old milk slops. I've had much nicer food at Peppina's.' She smelt of hay and was covered with dust and straw, and suddenly Silja was so overwhelmed with joy at having her home again that she had to cry in sympathy. When they had both calmed down and hugged each other so that their ribs hurt, Sissela told Silja about her day.

She had gone home with them in the Vackerbacka cart, and she had been playing all day with Peppina. They had sat in a ditch where it was dry and warm, nothing but the sky and stems of grass above them. No one could see them, and they had not answered when the others had called, because when no one sees you then you don't really *exist*, do you?

'Peppina,' said Sissela, 'has her hair very short so that it doesn't hurt when she has it combed. And then we tried to ride Piggywig, their great big pig, but it just threw us off and knocked us over with its snout and laughed at us with short little sounds from right down in its stomach. And then we ate as much as we liked from their garden, all the bird-damaged berries and snail-eaten things, and peas and carrots. I brought a carrot for you,' said Sissela, foraging among her flowers. 'And then I taught them to play the gold-crown game, and when I said it was all about Sola, Queen of Tulavall, they taught me another game called the Sola game, but they didn't know she was a queen. But their mother said that she had played it when she was little, and her mother and grandmother had played it when they were small.'

'But how did you come to be so silly as to play the gold-crown game with burrs!' said Silja.

"Because they stick so well. Aren't they grand? But do you want to hear about the Sola game? We can play it later when Sanna comes home. I've got a carrot for her, too, I think, and when I asked her for permission, Peppina said take the whole garden. One person is Mistress Sola and another Wolf and all the others are lambs and sheep. We could have the Blomfors lot, too. And Mistress Sola goes out and wanders around with her staff in her hand, the flock behind her in a long line. And then we meet Wolf. Then Mistress Sola thumps her staff on the ground and sings, and then we all sing, and she builds – in the air – and we help her:

"Mistress Sola stakes out the hop-field
between the Wolf and her sheep.
Firm as a sail,
slippery as glass.
No bird flies overhead
No snake creeps below
Water-tight
sky-high
and even higher.
Little stake, big stake, cross above all my tasses!"

'They call sheep "tasses" there, and call out "Tass, tass" to them. But all the time, Wolf is howling outside and mocking us, louder and louder, the louder we sing, and he says: "Is that anything, that?" And then we make a roof with turf and birch-bark and silver and gold, grander and grander, and Mistress Sola makes a copper gate between two sticks she thrusts into the ground, or in the cracks between the boards if we're playing indoors. But when the gate is ready, we can't see out, so we don't see when Wolf turns himself into an old woman. The old woman bangs on the copper gate and asks to be given a lamb, and she is so miserable that Mistress Sola gives her one and says: "Look after it well."

'Then the old woman goes away and hides it, and comes back and begs for another one, and then she does it again and again, and each time Mistress Sola says: "But what happened to the last one I gave you?" and the old woman has to think up something different each time; that it saw its reflection in the well and fell in and drowned or something. But when Mistress Sola hasn't any tasses left, she goes out through the copper gate to look for them and cries: "Taaaaasssssses! Taaaaaassssssses! Taaaaassssses!" The old woman promises to show her where they are, but lures Mistress Sola into the bath-house, and in the bath-house we are all turned into sheep, standing in a circle with our heads together and our arms round each other, and when Mistress Sola crawls into the bath-house, we fall on her and bury her beneath us.'

One day when Sanna came home, she was looking more serious than usual, and Silja and Sissela, who had been deep in a violent squabble over whose turn it was to wash up, stopped the moment they saw her.

'Klockarback-Fia came to the pottery today and asked to speak to me, and she said mamma must go away for a while to rest. Mamma has given her money for me for the rent for three whole months.'

They stared at her.

'Can't she rest here . . . if we look after her?'

'No, because she's still too weak. She can't cope with being here.'

'Where's she going?' That was Sissela. 'And is she going alone? Can't we go with her and help her?'

'No.'

'When's she going?'

Sanna said quietly, her voice thick: 'She went yesterday. Fia said it would have upset her too much to say goodbye to us.'

Fat tears immediately flowed from Sissela's eyes, and Silja rushed out. Someone in the yard stretched out a hand. 'And where are you off to in such a hurry?' But she rushed on so quickly that there was not even time for a pat on the head. She ran as fast as she could, and her chest hurt, not like a knife, but more like a corkscrew being turned for every breath she took. She ran along Longsand towards World's End, but there were some boys there. They were paddling, their trousers rolled up as high as possible, and they were brandishing sticks and shouting. They had prisoners on a raft they were pulling along behind them. Silja had often been the prisoner in games like that, when Stefan was younger – she turned and ran up towards town again, wishing that for at least one minute she could see Bonadea. She raced along the streets, and when she met people she knew, she did her best to appear to be on an important errand and so could not possibly stop. She ran on for what she thought seemed like several years, slowing down now and again when she got a stitch in her side, but not daring to stop altogether, because the ground was crackling beneath her like fresh ice, and black cracks kept appearing, hooking round her feet.

But then she came to West Wood, where mamma had stood shivering one night in the damp and the agony of waiting. There her tears caught up with her. She flung herself down in the green shade and the world might well come to an end for all she cared, as long as she could weep away her anguish first.

That was where old Mother Coriander found her when she came to hang up her washing. She stood there looking at her, blinking with compassion, but all she said was : 'Well, goodness me, what's grieving you so bad, then, eh?'

Silja's face was flushed and swollen, the whites of her eyes red, too, and she always got a wreath of red patches on her forehead when she cried. Now she was so unhappy that she had to talk to someone, to anyone, or to the next person to come along. She even forgot that she had always felt the greatest of respect for old Mother Coriander.

'Mamma's not coming back any more,' she said. 'She's gone away because she can't cooooooo-ope with us . . .'

When it had been said out aloud, she was so ashamed that she had to hide her face again. If mamma had gone away for any other reason whatsoever, Silja and her sisters would have striven and sacrificed themselves to get her back again. But when they themselves were the reason, there was nothing they could do.

Old Mother Coriander looked at her with her winking friendly little eyes, horse-shoe wrinkles appearing on her forehead as always when she was thinking. Then she sat down on a stone beside Silja and handed her a handkerchief. There was the smell of clean linen all round her. 'Has it never happened,' she said, 'that you failed in something you wanted very much?' That you couldn't cope although you did your very best?'

Silja had to stop crying in order to think. 'Yes, on the ice,' she said. 'When I went out too far with Sissela, and we might have died. But then Krullasse helped us in another direction instead, and we became friends,' she said, blowing her nose so that it bubbled.

Mother Coriander saw so many people coming and going from her place in West Wood. 'It could be that perhaps your mother has found a friend to help her,' she said.

Silja sat quite still.

'Few people can live through a whole life without help.'

Silja went on sitting still. She had hoped for the kind of consolation for her misery that was like being rocked in someone's arms, the kind that takes away all sorrows and burdens. She had hoped to hear that it was neither Sissela's nor Sanna's nor pappa's nor her fault that things had gone as they had. What Mother Coriander had said was only consoling if you were able to think it all out. She did her best. She remembered the strange man they had met that early morning, the one who had called mamma Emmeline. She remembered pappa's story about the bird.

Suddenly she jumped up and handed the handkerchief back to Mother Coriander. She began to run along the streets to get back to Sissela as quickly as possible and hug her and rock her in her arms and say that it wasn't her fault.

FIVE
Arcanum

In the evening of the same day that the stone had floated, Bonadea followed Jakem down into Gripander House cellar. Jakem was carrying an armful of long logs and a lantern suspended from his little finger. He walked sideways between the walls and his shadow made the cellar doubly dark and difficult. Bonadea lagged behind, her heart beating right up in her throat and her mouth dry and sticky.

She heard Jakem kick at a door and grunt. Then the door opened and he vanished, wood, lantern and all, into a dim reddish chasm – or that was what it seemed like as she fumbled her way along the uneven passage. But it was Herr Turiam's workroom. It was quite big and full of things, but there was an empty space round the chimney piece, which was the most enormous one she had ever seen, bricked in ledges, with iron shutters. On one ledge, a heap of embers was winking with scarlet eyes. On another was a kind of metal stove – like a tower, standing on feet and with circular openings, and pipes that led in loops out of the sides and in again.

Over by the desk, Herr Turiam said something impatient in that foreign language that was perhaps German or Latin or Brakotchetish, and Jakem flung down the wood and stumped out. Bonadea stayed over by the door. Herr Turiam had asked her to come, but he took no notice of her at all now. He was writing with a rasping sound over in his corner by the light of candles in tall candlesticks. He muttered to himself, then threw his pen to the floor and picked up another. She had plenty of time to look round.

She reckoned the cellar must lie in the corner facing on to Market Square and Clapper Street. There were windows right up under the ceiling, at street level. She knew that on the outside they were protected by grids. On the inside, Herr Turiam had stretched white material across them to stop people looking in, at the same time letting in the daylight. Now at night, they were covered with black shrouds.

There were several tables in the room, all covered with bottles and pots and jars of clay and glass and metal. There were books and paper and apparatus, too, and the skull of a horse in one corner. On the walls between the shelves that were also crowded with things, were several large pictures. The most splendid of them was coloured green and gold, depicting a monster, perhaps a lion, or a wolf, in the process of devouring the sun.

Herr Turiam stabbed with his pen and put it down, muttering, putting his hand over his eyes and then scratching his head with both hands. When he turned round and caught sight of her, he said: 'Oh, so you're here, are you?'

He was wearing a long dark gown like a monk's habit or a long working smock. It looked old-fashioned and strange, but was probably pleasant to wear while keeping watch in the damp of the cellar all night. She shivered, changed foot and curled up her toes.

'Haven't you got anything on your feet?' Herr Turiam said. He had told her to dress warmly, so she was wearing the 'wolf' she had borrowed from Black Sea Sailor. It smelt of tar and fish and was as long as a coat on her, the sleeves rolled up. She shook her head. 'I came here barefoot.'

He hunted out a peculiar pair of shoes from a chest. They were made of red felt with leather figures in green and turquoise stuck on them. They had thick soles of rawhide and were only slightly too large. He said they came from the country of Mithonggatka, far, far away, half-way to the sky,

where he had once many years ago studied the art of wingless flying. 'Is that farther away than Barbidel country?' said Bonadea. But he had never heard of Barbidel country. 'Did you learn to fly?' said Bonadea. He muttered and said that he had got as far as managing to get off the ground. 'But Gunna was better at it.'

'Who's Gunna?' she asked.

'My housekeeper,' he said.

Bonadea felt better when her feet warmed up. When Herr Turiam had put wood on the embers and the fire had burnt up, she saw something glimmering on the front of her sweater. A thread of curled copper. One of the hairs from Black Sea Sailor's beard. She felt that meant that he was almost there, too, so she took courage and dared turn her back on the black wrought-iron door in the corner beyond the stove that seemed to lead straight down into the underworld.

Herr Turiam searched among his flasks and vessels, saying that he was going to do the simple trinity test, to see if it made any difference who stirred. She had to sit on a stool by the fire and hold a jar on her lap. He lifted up a pair of trembling scales. In one bowl he poured a substance that looked like salt. 'It's salt,' he said, when she asked. Then he weighed out an equal quantity of sulphur and quicksilver and poured them into her jar. 'Now stir as evenly and smoothly as you can, counter-clockwise. Now you're stirring the elements of fire and water and matter. And by stirring, they are blended with the fourth element, air.'

It smelt nasty, scorching and smarting so that her nose began to run. She stirred as best she could. Meanwhile, he hurriedly weighed out and measured things. He poured water into a pot and put it on to a three-legged stand above the fire, mumbling to himself. He reminded her a little of Anna Siili making gingerbread biscuits.

'Can just anyone make gold?' she said respectfully. 'If you've got the right recipe?'

'No,' he said, frowning as if he had been disturbed. Then his brow cleared, as he obviously liked talking. 'Gold is heavenly fire frozen and dead – but even in that dead state, it is noble, the most noble of all metals. It neither rusts nor acquires verdigris. We can melt it and mix it with other metals, we can beat it and cast it into a thousand forms, but we cannot burn it, for fire has no power to burn fire . . . so it is impossible to make gold with only earthly materials, either by physics or chemistry or any of the exact sciences.'

'But what about sorcery?'

'With internal magical fire. With the willpower that one either possesses or doesn't. Without that fire, no spirits can be constrained. But naturally a number of external means of assistance are also required, and I haven't yet managed to come to the perfect result.'

His eyes were now burning and strong again, glittering on each side of his shadowing nose. She dared not meet them. 'You have to weigh and try out,' he said. 'Try again and again. Mixing the unearthly with the earthly, increasing your knowledge, burrowing your way forward through the great mountains of the night.' He bent forward as if his nose were a divining-rod. 'Knowledge in alchemy is the gateway to the Kingdom of Colour, to the Kingdom of Words – where cannot one reach by putting together the right words! I remember when I was a beginner and had to learn for my homework all the different names for quicksilver: silver-water, the divine dew, moon-tears, milk-of-a-black-cow ... I had no idea what the point was at the time.'

Bonadea's arm began to tire. She didn't understand everything he was talking about, far from it, and in the long run could not follow what he was saying, as it was beginning to get so hot in there. Her neck ached from sitting still, her face burned, and she thought: 'He's rambling.' Then she thought that perhaps he was like Black Sea Sailor when he went off tramping, talking a whole lot of funny nonsense to avoid all the questions.

Herr Turiam talked about the salamanders that lived in the fire. 'They're shy. They prefer to hide themselves in their own element. Perhaps they'll show themselves to you because you're a child. If there are inhabitants on the sun, then I think they must be some kind of salamanders.'

The glow from the fire grew before her eyes into a shining mountain. She was stirring more and more sluggishly, and after she had stared for a long time, she saw glimpses of swift movements, as if bodies were enjoying themselves hurtling from cliff to cliff. On that occasion it was no more than a swift glimpse. because Herr Turiam took the jar from her. He looked at the contents and mumbled that it was the right colour. 'Let's go on.' He took dried leaves out of a little metal box and powdered them in between his hands into the mass of earth and water and fire and air she had mixed. 'More earth,' he mumbled. Then he threw it all into the fire. She heard him call out in a mighty voice, and a black cloud of smoke billowed out. The room grew so dark that she could see neither walls nor roof, and the glow of the fire was suspended, dark and dull, contained like a piece of clothing hanging out to dry.

'Come,' said Herr Turiam, taking her hand. 'We must move closer.' They moved closer, until the chimney stopped them. 'Take hold and haul yourself up,' he said, and Bonadea did so, surprised that the edge was so high and the brickwork so rough and uneven. It wasn't a chimney but a cliff edge. She felt dry moss and sharp tufts of grass under her fingers and the smell of dry mountain plants prickled her nose. She heard Herr Turiam panting behind her and thought that climbing like this must be twice as difficult for an old man with stiff legs like him. She stretched and heaved and got her knees up high and clambered over the edge.

Herr Turiam stretched out his thin hand and she dug her heels in and hauled him up the last bit.

They were standing on a plain where the rocky projections and hillocks and thickets rose black against the red sky. In the middle of all that red was a heavy moon of gold. 'Come,' said Herr Turiam when he had got his breath back, and together they began to walk towards the moon.

But the ground was uneven, full of crevices, and the dusky light was deluding. Streams they couldn't see tumbled along at the bottom of the deepest ravines. They were scratched by thorny briars and kept stumbling over things. Herr Turiam stopped now and again, looked round, and drew circles and signs in the air with his stick. Then he said with satisfaction: 'Aha!' They came out on to a winding path.

Now they moved on more quickly. But the moon had sunk from sight when they finally reached the horizon, which was nothing but a cliff, a chasm, where the red light was playing, but otherwise nothing else; well, some kind of bats with red eyes were swirling uneasily back and forth. When Bonadea turned round, she saw the rocky plain dark behind her, and the stars had begun to come out above.

She was tired now and her legs were aching. But Herr Turiam allowed them no rest. Cautiously, muttering and mumbling, he lowered himself over the edge. 'Come,' he said impatiently when Bonadea hesitated. There was a crack there and when she fumbled round, she found holds for her hands and feet. But they were shallow and insufficient and the palms of her hands and the soles of her feet grew sweaty. She pressed herself against the cliff, but it seemed to be moving, leaning over, and the next moment she would fall off it from her own weight – and the next moment she clung on as before, and the next, and the next, while the aching of her taxed body seemed like a crocheted net.

'How you do dawdle!' said Herr Turiam from below her. 'There are only a few more steps. Let go. Let yourself slide.'

She thought that nothing on earth would induce her to let go, but at that moment she did, and slid all the same. 'There we are,' said Herr Turiam, and she was there, gasping, her skin grazed, standing in front of him on a ledge.

He began to walk along the ledge as calmly as if back in his room, and then vanished round a corner. Afraid of being left alone, Bonadea hurried after him as fast as she dared. 'Don't rush so,' he said when she bumped straight into him on the other side of the projection. 'Listen now. Where this ledge widens next, there's the fire-vulture's nest. We must get an egg from it. The parent birds are out hunting at the moment. If they come back before we've got away, they'll attack us and try to tip us over into the ravine. Climb up into the nest and take one of the eggs. There are usually two. Put it into your skirt pocket. Mind you don't break it. I'll keep watch, and if the vultures come, I'll do my best to fend them off.'

She nodded. She scrambled along the ledge and they came to the vultures' nest. It was as large as three haystacks, a huge pile of branches and thorny twigs that stank of old and more recent garbage and bones. In a hollow at the top lay two shining glowing scarlet eggs. She crawled into the swaying stack, scratching herself and choking over the putrid smell. Then she heard a shrill screech out there in the air, and another, and another, and the swishing sound of wings. 'Hurry!' shouted Herr Turiam, and she crawled on as quickly as she could. Shadows swept over her and she hunched up, not daring to look round. Then she heard a loud crack, and another, then screeches and bangs like sharp shots. When she had the egg in her pocket, she turned round.

Herr Turiam was standing below the nest on the narrow space between the steep rock-face and the scarlet void, striking out at the birds with a cracking whip. She slid down to him. 'Go on ahead,' he commanded, and she wriggled past him. He followed, close behind, slashing the whip all round them, above them and to the sides, and the draught from it and the ragged wings of the vultures swirled round them. Bonadea's hair whipped in her face. She had caught a glimpse of the vultures' legs, as thick as a man's arm, the claws like butcher's hooks, except their colour, and they shone like a blend of gold and copper.

Then they were back in the ravine and climbing upwards, climbing, climbing. 'Mind the egg!' said Herr Turiam breathlessly, and Bonadea stopped, dizzy and despairing because what they now had ahead of them was where she had to cling on with the whole of her body and she could not possibly go any further without breaking the egg in her pocket. But then she saw something, a curly rope of reddish-gold copper, as firm and steady as a ladder, wedged into a crevice. She grasped it and hauled herself up from ledge to ledge along it. It had not been there on the way down. When she got to the top and turned round, it had gone again, and Herr Turiam had to climb up without assistance, one hand grasping the whip with which he swung and slashed around.

'I can't go any further now,' said Bonadea, when Herr Turiam had got up. She was trembling all over with exhaustion, the plain was black, and the sky was black, but the stars were white and thick. 'You must take one more step,' said Herr Turiam quite calmly, dragging her with him into the darkness. She stumbled and hit her leg. 'You can sit down now,' he said, and she sat down with a bump. 'But mind the egg!' he cried out anxiously.

The air was much warmer now, quite still all round them. The stars had vanished. 'Are we in a cave?' she said. He did not reply, but she heard him fumbling round. Then he struck a match and she saw they were in his work-cellar. She was sitting on the floor beside the stool she had stumbled over, and the fire was almost dead beneath its covering of ash. Herr Turiam lit several candles and gazed at her not without pleasure. 'Have you got the egg?'

She handed it to him with a shaking hand.

'We managed it this time,' he said.

She gasped and swallowed before she managed to blurt out: 'Have you tried before?'

'Many a time. Drink this, and you'll feel better. It's Gunna's rhubarb wine. Nothing to worry about, not even strong, but take it in sips. I've tried on my own and was nearly dragged down into the ravine, and I practised with the whip on bats until I could defend myself properly. I've tried with Gunna, too, but that was before she got fat. But she left the egg there when the vultures came, tearing off her apron and even trying to defend me with it.' He laughed a mocking, chuckling little laugh. 'Another time she already had the egg in her hand and used it as a weapon. But she didn't know how to throw and just broke it against the cliff. I was really angry with her that time.'

Bonadea drank the wine as he had told her to, in small sips, and it spread warmth and sweetness all through her.

'One can't try too often, you see, because the vultures would be frightened off and go elsewhere. One has to be patient for five years, or ten years between each attempt.'

Bonadea was still sitting on the floor with her arms round her knees. 'Were we actually *here* all the time, then?' she said. 'Or were we really out, out of doors, somewhere else? And what was it you cried out?'

'Hasala! Disla! Tuga! That's such an old formula that no one knows what it means any longer. I learnt it from my godfather. But it's like that with formulas, and even if their meaning has disappeared, they're effective if they're said at the right moment and with the right solemnity. As far as your first question is concerned, there's no definite answer to that. We live in several worlds at the same time. But they obscure each other. They mostly obscure each other.'

As he was talking, he was easing the egg into a wide-topped glass bottle. He put a lid over it that wasn't really tight, explaining that if the pressure inside the bottle became too great, it would be better for the lid to blow off than for the bottle to explode. He opened a door in the tower-like stove and placed the bottle inside, just as one puts dough aside to rise. He stoked up the fire below the stove and said: 'Now I must keep an even temperature for ninety days, then perhaps it'll hatch out.'

She must have fallen asleep where she was, because she woke suddenly to the twitter of birds. The same red glow of light and gloomy duskiness she had seen when she had first come were still there, but the clear notes of the blackbird outside told her that the night was over. 'Give that to me now,' said Herr Turiam, and then she noticed that she had been holding a metal bowl in her cupped hands.

'It's quite warm,' said Herr Turiam. 'Now let's see,' and he put a few dried leaves into the bowl. They slowly straightened themselves out in the warmth from the metal, a fine scent rising from them. He leant over and watched them tensely, but when she yawned, he suddenly turned to her. 'Go to bed now,' he said. 'Come back again when the sun goes down.'

Later on, when she thought about her time at Gripander House, she could remember only a few of the evenings properly. The others had all merged together into a scarlet mist, stinging curling vapours rising to the ceiling and sinking again as dampness, charcoal fires keeping the heat even, but lacking the living sounds of a wood-fire. Once when the whole cellar was thick with steam from a cauldron, Herr Turiam said:

'That's not good for my books.' He put the lid on the pan and through the lid threaded a pipe, then joined the pipe to other pipes leading into the chimney. 'Not that books mean much nowadays – except as company, as reminders of others who have striven and experimented. The greatest wisdom can never be learnt from texts, but naturally they're important for beginners.'

Bonadea looked at them and wished that Silja were there. Silja liked books so much. They were big books, some of them handwritten and worn at the edges. They were called things like *Paragranum, Paramirum, On the Face of the Moon* and *Tabula Smaragdina.* Most of them were in incomprehensible language, written in letters she did not recognize. But they had strange and wonderful pictures, diagrams or magic formulas. She buried herself in them until Herr Turiam called to her.

He had taken the lid off the pan and the substance in it had now boiled into a dark-brown dough that he scraped out. 'More air this time,' he said. 'Blow on it. Blow as hard as you can. I don't know where you'll get to this time, or what you'll see, and I'll leave it to your own judgement to decide what you bring back with you.'

He scraped the dough down into the embers. She blew until

she was dizzy. She pressed on her hands and went on blowing, and exactly like the last time, the whole room vanished into black smoke, into black darkness. She grasped the edge and closed her eyes, and when she looked up again she was on a plain, but not the same one as last time.

The previous plain had aroused her curiosity and her desire to explore. If only it had been daytime, she had thought then, she would have run round, splashed in the running streams, explored the glades and ravines. But this plain was gloomy and horrible. The craggy ledges outlined against the sky were not cliffs but ruins of great houses, the streams sluggish, their waters black and thick, covered with dust like fur. Underfoot was nothing but wreckage and rubbish. As she walked and walked, there was no sign of life, not a single green stalk, no earth even, just ash. When the billowing darkness gradually lifted, she thought she could see ghosts moving about among the crumbling walls and she hurried towards them for company. But they weren't even ghosts, only swirling fumes that stank.

The only thing that rose above the flatness of the plain was a mound, and she made her way towards it because she did not know where else to go. But when she approached it, it exploded with a growling sound that shook the ground. She would have been knocked over if she hadn't been walking just slightly above ground, a fact she noticed only then. Thick glowing embers poured out, and how beautiful it was! With relief and delight, she watched the desolate heaps of filth being covered with gliding red gold, slowly solidifying into crests and ridges.

But the heat belching out of the burning mountain was so strong that she had to turn away to protect her face. She was forced to flee as fast as she could, and the roaring from the earth grew louder, the mound exploding more and more and rising higher – the whole plain tilting, with glowing cracks racing through it like lightning streaking across the sky.

She fled back as quickly as she could, noticing with relief that she was flying, the ground rolling beneath her in waves like a shaken rug, and the foul runnels of dirt turning to steam. She flew through the stinging air currents right out to the edge, and just as she lowered herself down over it, she turned and saw the devastated landscape burst into bloom like a single glorious glowing rose.

'You're empty-handed?' said Herr Turiam, neither disappointed nor angry, but tensely questioning. She took a deep trembling breath, her heart fluttering, and tears in her eyes, her hair smelling of burning. 'I hadn't time.' He passed her a scoop of water and after she had drunk, she told him what she had seen. 'But I didn't have time to bring anything with me.'

'You had time to *see*,' he said. 'You've given me your description. And you were away quite a long time. That'll do for tonight.'

Dizzy with fatigue, she made her way out, staggering on the stairs and stumbling over the smooth floor. It was already light, the wind sweeping in through the open kitchen window. She went out and wiped her feet on the grass. And her hands. Then she rubbed her face with her dewy hands.

She had made it an early morning habit, after her part in the night's work was over, to go out into the garden and pick dandelions in the ruins of the brewery. On the craggy heaps of stones, among fallen remains of walls and vaults and steps that led up into nowhere, were grass and flowers, and young trees growing; aspen, pussy-willow, maple and a few birches, all in a circle forming a glade. She made chains with dandelion stalks and hung them up in the trees, where they swayed in the wind. When they died, they sometimes broke. But every morning she made some more. The whole glade gradually became surrounded by swinging pendants.

She liked sitting among the airy trees that were so close to each other that she could see neither the hedges nor the railings behind them, and she could imagine she was in the middle of the forest. She thought about the glade during the long nights when sleep gradually started overcoming her, making her shiver and freeze, when her work was to stir and mix and grind, or watch the seething brews that had to be boiled over and over again, or when she simply had to be to hand and wait until her eyes started smarting and her hands fumbling. Sometimes when she had been awake for a long time, the sky seemed faded, poor shreds that could be seen through the thick foliage of the garden. Sometimes the new day's sunlight winked through the trees, the shadows like transparent tents, and she was so tired that she could hardly feel the ground beneath her feet everything she touched feeling unreal.

One morning she found the *Pike* and the *Emmanuel* in the pond among the pond weed and water-lilies. They looked so lost and lonely as they lay out there, as if they had strayed far away. The *Emmanuel* had lost her masts and was floating upside-down.

As the sun rose higher and voices began to make themselves heard from the streets and the square and the houses over the hedges, her head usually began to feel heavy and she went off to bed. Herr Turiam, she thought, never slept.

As she lay on her bed with the window creaking on the hook, gulls screaming, sparrows chattering and the wind blowing in, she heard words and sentences in Herr Turiam's voice penetrating right into her dreams.

'Some scientists believe that the origins of life should be sought in the sea. They say that the earth was once covered with sea, shining masses of water hovering and roaring, whipped by storms into foaming mountains and swaying high towards the moon, which pulled its tidal train as regularly as the sigh of a heart – huge mountains of water rolling round the earth. And in that water, the first signs of the mote of life is supposed to have appeared. But I say the origin of life is fire.'

SIX
On the Hill

It was a strange story Bonadea heard when, after so many weeks, she once again came to Bulder's at Gold Crown corner. No one was home at the Halters'. Pappa had begun wandering about, the neighbours said, Stefan was at sea, and the girls had gone to the pottery. 'And I suppose you've heard about their mother? No, haven't you heard that Mother Halter . . . and you such good friends with the girls, and all . . .'

The little Walloon lacemaker said: 'I never would've thought she'd be so flighty and just go off like that,' pursing her upper lip as she said it, as if she had something nice in her mouth. 'But perhaps she's been changed by her illness . . .'

'To have a rest, they call it . . . for health reasons . . . I suppose she thinks she's one of the gentry. Well, I was that poorly after my last babe, I could've rested for a year,' said Mother Birgersson, but she was interrupted by Mother Kröpelin: 'Makes you wonder if the money she paid the rent with in advance was got in some fine way . . .'

They shook their heads. In the pleasure of being able to discuss Mother Halter all over again, they had quite forgotten that they had meant to ask Bonadea where she had been for so long.

'If you ask *me*,' they said. 'She didn't go alone. But love's round like a ball, and anyone can win a prize if he's the only competitor, can't he now?'

'Shame on you, all of you!' said Mother Blomfors, her sturdy arms akimbo. She had come barefoot across the grass, so they had not heard her. 'She was expecting to come into some money, that's what she told *me*, and as things are for her, we shouldn't grudge her even a hare's foot. Oh, Bonadea, what a good thing you've come. You can hold the babe for me, while I get the food ready.'

'All I say is that I know where I'll go for health reasons, and that's to Rummelbacken,' moaned Mother Birgirsson, and they all laughed, because Rummelbacken was where the new cemetery was.

'I thought,' said Mother Blomfors, when they were in her kitchen, 'you might as well wait for the girls here at my place. They'll be back soon. I've promised them dinner today.'

'We're going to have stewed plums!' shouted Uffe, who was lying on the floor under the bed trying to saw a trapdoor into the floor.

Mother Blomfors was jigging absently with little Fi on her arm, yodelling: 'Mamma's little angel, mamma's little oomsie-lool.' Then she abruptly dumped her into Bonadea's arms. 'Mother Halter's gone away with a man,' she said. 'I might as well tell you what's what, because you'll soon hear more than you need to about it all. She went away because she was half-dead and was having a difficult time in many ways, and he was the only person she could turn to for help. Yes, for money, too. I don't know if it was the right or the wrong thing to do, but most things you do are a bit of both, to the delight of the tittle-tattlers. Anyhow, I tell everyone I can that it's an inheritance – anyone can be left money, and they've no need to preen themselves.'

Mother Blomfors tossed the buckled metal plates on to the table as if she were throwing flat stones on the water. She took the cod out of the oven and began to bone a bit for Fi. Then the children crowded in, Beata, Rosmarie, Åka and little Petrus. Uffe crept out and there was bustle and commotion as usual, shaggy heads surging at all levels above the floor. Sanna and Silja staggered in with a pail of soft and ready-puddled clay between them, Sissela behind them, clay all over her arms, hands and cheeks and with a clay hen she had made herself, wrapped in huge maple leaves like a golden loaf in her arm.

'Where's pappa?' said Rosmarie.

'He's at work. Some chairs have got worm in their legs and have to be repaired for the Kattestedt wedding.'

Bonadea fed Fi with fish and potatoes, and in between ate as much as she could herself from the same spoon. The stewed plums were put in the middle of the table. When they had finished their fish, each one licked the plate and piled it up with stewed plums, then began shooting at the milk mugs by spitting stones at them. Sissela laughed loudly and did the same. Silja was sharing a chair with her – the other children were all squashed along the long bench – and she sat looking at Bonadea, fidgeting and making faces. There was so much she wanted to know. Sanna finished her meal like an adult and placed all her fishbones neatly on the table by her plate, her stones alongside them. She offered to help with the dishes when everyone had finished.

As the sun was setting, Sanna, Silja, Sissela and Bonadea were sitting up on the hill. Sissela was making pots from the clay from the pottery, to have when they played at the Stone Age, squeezing a thick sausage in her left hand, putting it on the rock and sticking her forefinger into it. When it had dried in the sun, it would hold berries, ten or so in each pot. Sanna was learning to make pots properly on a wheel, as well as plates and dishes, and she smiled at her. But she did not interfere with Sissela's method of working, because little children should be left alone with their ploys. Silja was making a wreath of grass stalks. Bonadea was holding Cacklehilda in her arms.

They had so much to ask and talk about that they didn't know where to begin, even feeling slightly like strangers. But all the same it was good to be together.

'I've got the bark-boats in the window for company,' said Bonadea.

'Is he nasty?' said Silja, quietly, meaning Herr Turiam.

'No,' said Bonadea. 'But difficult.'

'I don't suppose there are lice there, anyhow,' said Sanna, and Bonadea laughed slightly. 'No.' Early that spring she had found a whole lot of birds under the shed in the baker's yard.

They were blackbirds mostly, and they had seemed almost dead. But she had bedded them down in wood-shavings up in her attic and they had revived. She had kept them up there until the weather grew warmer, feeding them on cold porridge. They had been full of small black fleas, not chicken lice, but real jumping fleas which had almost eaten her alive, and she hadn't been able to get rid of them, so had been forced to move.

The other girls laughed too. 'Silja had nits again for a while,' said Sanna. 'They stick to her so well. I think she must have sweet blood. So she had to go round with sabadilla on her head, but Aunt Lingon says she should walk naked three times round the garden with a crown of hay on her head and a mirror in her hand.'

They laughed gratefully at Aunt Lingon's good advice.

'But what do you *do* at Gripander House?' said Sanna, straight to the point at last. She and Silja were respectful but obstinately inquisitive, thinking that Bonadea seemed more distant from them now she was sitting there saying nothing, than when she was away and they had been able to converse with her in their thoughts.

'It is difficult? You look as pale as . . .'

Bonadea was usually brown most of the year, starting as early as March and her tan staying right up until Christmas. But now she had faded.

'. . . and blue round your eyes, as if someone had drawn sooty thumbs under them.'

'I'm up late at nights.'

Sissela sighed with envy. 'Sanna's much stricter with me than mamma was,' she said. 'I have to go to bed in the middle of the day almost.'

'Tell us something,' said the girls, but Bonadea did not know which words to use. 'I just help,' she said. 'It's not at all like what we thought. Sometimes it's slow and boring.' There were nights she could not remember at all, except for Herr Turiam's tense face, his eyes, attentively watching the progress of an experiment. She found that to describe what he was like properly, she had to say he had blue-black hair that went straight back from his forehead, that he was covered with brilliant blue scales all over, and that much of what she had experienced was difficult to keep track of.

'You've been dreaming!' said Sanna.

'I was in a long corridor and there were lots of doors with glass in them, that kind of rough knobbly glass you can't see through, and I had to find my way out of the right door, because someone was after me,' said Bonadea. 'But I never would have found it if Silja hadn't stood out on the steps and held her thumb against the glass so that I saw it. It was like a tiny white new potato.'

As she told her story, she was very grateful to Silja, who had saved her that time, but Silja said: 'That was the day when you were in the hall and there *was* only one door.'

'Perhaps I dreamt it,' Bonadea admitted. So she told them about the salamanders. She really had seen them one night, playing in the embers like kittens, rolling round biting each other's tails. Their heads were shaped rather like a cat's, if you wiped off the ears, and they had glittering crests along their backs. When she had seen them, she had remembered the little dancing fire-woman she had once seen long long ago in Anna Siili's bakery, and when she told Herr Turiam, he said: 'That doesn't surprise me. Earthly image for earthly mind.'

'That sounds funny,' said Sanna, and Bonadea replied: 'Yes,' then she turned away from them and looked around. It was so good to have the sky above you, not a ceiling or leafy trees. It was quite still, and the shining pale evening sea was moving towards the shore, as if lifting the whole country silently and freely, higher and higher towards the sky. And the sky was another pale blue sea, but with no islands, no ships and no end.

'How are things with you, then?' said Bonadea.

Silja sighed, but Sanna drawled: 'All right. I mean we're managing. And you can come and live with us, when you can get away. You can have Stefan's den as you like attics, because he's not fishing any more. He's signed on to a steamer, the *Postillion.* He says it's grander to be on a steamer. He sails between Stockholm and Helsinki and Reval and Petersburg, and he doesn't want to come home at the moment, because Bulder is horrible to him and torments him when they meet.'

Sissela sat up and paid attention. The children down in the yard had begun to play the Sola game. She quickly washed the worst of the clay off herself in a crevice full of water and rushed off down the hill, her arms swinging. She was proud of

introducing a new and popular game and always wanted to join in when they played it.

'What do you want, Mistress Sola?' said the voice from down in the yard.

'I want to borrow a tass.' Uffe was the wolf.

'What did you do with the last one I gave you?'

'He ran against a rock and broke his leg.'

'Baaa! Baaa Baaa!' shouted Sissela, pushing her way into the crowd. Rosmarie cried out: 'You can't come into Mistress Sola's yard, because the roof's on and the gate closed. You must wait until next time.'

'I can, I can, I'm a ghost of a sheep!' cried Sissela, and as they all knew how pointless it was squabbling with her, because she always had an answer and never gave in, she was allowed to join them.

'I want to borrow a tass . . . because the last one ran away up the hill . . .'

The wolf got Beata this time and shoved her behind the lilac bushes, then again thumped on Mistress Sola's gateway: 'The one I got last time had to sit on a glass mountain and wait to get married . . .'

They laughed down there, but Beata shouted angrily back. Silja's face seemed hollow and her voice uncertain, so she had to speak very quietly to get it out at all: 'I think it's awful, this game . . . when Mistress Sola in the end gets buried alive by her own children . . .'

'By her own sheep,' corrected Sanna.

'She does her best all the time, and yet it goes wrong.'

'Things go wrong for everyone sooner or later,' said Sanna, a little dryly. 'If you mean things go wrong when you die.'

'I mean because she was cheated!' snapped Silja.

'I think it's a fine game just because of that, I mean, because she *does* do her best, right to the end. It'd be awful if she'd also become greedy and suspicious and miserly and just sat there hiding behind her copper gateway. Then you just couldn't like her,' said Bonadea.

Because she saw Silja's chin trembling, Sanna said comfortingly: 'It's such an old game . . . perhaps the end got forgotten.'

'I must go back now,' said Bonadea.

'Can we come with you?'

She hesitated, but then said yes, because the urge to go back was much stronger than she had thought it would be. She felt it so much that she grew tired. So she walked rather slowly across the hill and down the gully. Golden rod was flowering in the crevices and the moss was dry underfoot. The tangles of bird-cherry were grey with cocoon webs. When they got down to Gold Crown Lane, the sea was again hidden by houses and trees. Bonadea walked with her head drooping, twisting a straw round and round and round.

When they came to the wall round the old churchyard, she

stopped: 'You can't come with me any longer.' She lifted Cacklehilda up and put her in Silja's arms. 'I'll come again one evening, if I can.'

'How long do you have to go on being there?'

'Don't know.'

Silja was going to say something else, but at that moment Herr Klingkors came striding between the graves, his face, usually so benign, red and angry. The girls retreated from the porch where they had been standing. They curtseyed, but he strode past without seeing them. Sanna and Silja watched him go. His shadow was so long across Church Square that it looked as if he were dragging a tail behind him. When they looked round again, Bonadea had gone. They ran along the wall and bumped into Storswarts Niklas. They asked him: 'Have you seen Bonadea?' But he replied: 'Wasn't she standing there talking to you?'

She was hiding behind the Morrstjärna family chapel, spelt Mååhrdstierna carved in stone letters on the gable, until she was sure they had gone. When she had asked Herr Turiam for permission to go and see her friends, he had been reluctant. He was afraid she would be too tired to be any use. But she told him that she was worried and that worrying scattered her thoughts, so she would be no use anyhow. Then he had shown her a secret passage running under the ruins of the brewery to the old churchyard, and he had asked her to take that way, but be careful not to be seen.

Behind Morrstjärna's chapel, there were nettles taller than herself, and tangled elderberry bushes and rowans and a cairn of large stones. There was a black hole there, too, like a well, and she plunged into it, fumbling along a projecting ledge until she found her lantern. She had matches in her pocket.

In the light of the lantern, the rocky walls threw shadows that made it look as if the passage suddenly came to an end. But she walked into the shadows. There were sharp bends down there, several of them, and in one place the roof had fallen in. She had to bend low and even so the damp rough rock scraped against the back of her neck. Her stomach stirred uneasily, but that was because it was chilly, not because she was afraid. She felt more at home there than in the cellar at Gripander House.

In one place, where the passage ran quite near the Tisla, the ground was so wet that her feet sank into it. Apart from prints of her own bare feet, she noticed prints of large shoes there.

Then she emerged below the ruins of the brewery, where the air was mild, where the leaves and chains of dandelion stalks hung still. She ate a few sorrel leaves and washed herself in the stream before going in.

There was nothing in the kitchen but buzzing flies. She made herself a sandwich. The whole house was quiet. She had no alternative but to put on her slippers and go down to the cellar.

Herr Turiam's door was there with the strip of light round it and more light coming through the keyhole. She opened it without knocking, as she had been told to. Everything in there was as usual – the firelight that turned the air itself red, the smell of strange scorched and blended substances, papers and objects in heaps everywhere and Herr Turiam in the corner at his desk. But standing in the middle of the floor was the housekeeper, her eyes glistening as if filled with tears. She glanced at Bonadea, but took no more notice of her. She said to Herr Turiam: 'The older and poorer you get, the greater the demands you make. You're like one of those suitors on the glass mountain, but now you've tried so many times and fallen down again halfway, you should realize you're not the chosen one.'

'You've been listening.'

'Of course,' she said. 'Ever since we first met I've been listening to you. But only recently have I been forced to do so in secret. I was the one who brought you here. I thought we could live in peace here in this country, and we could have done, too, if only you'd kept your meddling fingers in check.'

'As soon as I discover the secret,' he began, but she interrupted him with a loud snort. He said passionately: 'No one can say I've failed as long as I haven't given up.'

'Time passes,' she said, 'and you're not your own master now. The person who lent you money will expect something for it. He's already threatening you. And I know he has power. If his patience runs out, it won't make any difference whether you've given up or not.'

Herr Turiam glared at her. 'I'm going to do the Eckartshausen experiment tonight.'

'No!' she exclaimed. 'That's dangerous. You'll end in an

asylum like Martinus Weis.'

'Quiet!' he snapped back. 'When time is short, you have to take short cuts.'

She lowered her head and her voice, muttering all the same: 'If only you'd let me help you. I've always been allowed to help you before. Why did you bring this wilful girl into it? She's just an extra mouth to feed. And if you destroy her with your short cuts, then you'll be lost yourself.'

'You know perfectly well why you can't help me any longer,' he said impatiently, 'Out you go, now.'

The housekeeper turned away from him. 'I'll hold out against you anyhow, as long as I have breath in my body. That can't be helped now, I like you so much, you old wretch,' she said and then left. She closed the door behind her remarkably quietly.

Herr Turiam thumped his fist hard down on the nearest table. But all the same, Bonadea found the courage to ask: 'Why can't she help you?'

'Because,' he said crossly, 'she's a faithful soul. She has thoughts only for *me*. She doesn't mind whether the work goes well or badly. If you want to succeed in these difficult matters, you have to use all your strength and forget yourself. Get out the *Parabrahm* book and look up the chapter called *Calling up Spirits* – it's somewhere near the end.'

He went and sat by the fire with his head in his hands, while

Bonadea searched. She took one of the wax candles to the shelf of thick handwritten books. She turned over the pages, reading a word here and a word there.

'The sun is the eye of life.'

'A person who concentrates all his willpower on a thought and directs it on to a definite goal, can if he fails, himself be killed by the force he has set in action. We find an illustration of this law when a person dies of grief over a frustrated hope.'

'Cornelius Agrippa says: make a powder of spermaceti, aloes, saffron and thyme, then sprinkle the blood of a hoopoe over it. If this paste is burnt on the graves of the dead, their ethereal forms will appear and perchance become visible.'

'Eckartshausen: Mix pulverized frankincense, fine flour and egg . . .'

'Here it is.'

He got up and took the book from her. 'What are we going to do?' she said cautiously.

'Call up the spirits of those who have gone further in knowledge than I have and taken their secret with them to the grave,' he said. 'Don't be afraid. Nothing will hurt you so long as you are not afraid. But we must use the stronger recipe. This one with egg and flour and rosewater won't do under present circumstances.'

Swiftly, he took down a number of small stone jars from a shelf and read half-aloud from the labels: 'hemlock, saffron, opium, mandragora . . . henbane, laburnam . . . yes, yes.' He weighed out equal portions of everything into a stone mortar and handed it to Bonadea. 'Grind it up fine, but mind it doesn't fly up into your eyes.'

As she was grinding with small careful movements, he poked about and extracted various objects, muttering: 'I've lived far too long on borrowed prospects of avarice. Why is gold so expensive? I know a country where the actual bedrock is streaked with gold, streaky like bacon. People there covered their roofs with gold for the sun to mirror itself in. But as a means of payment they used small round shells. And they were plundered, yes, yes, they were destroyed by the same foolishness that I am forced to serve, for it is stronger than I am.'

'Do you mean you don't really *want* to make gold?' said Bonadea.

'Not dead gold, no. It's the living gold I want to have. The arcanum of fire. The greatest knowledge, the cure for man's sickness and evil, at any price. But I have promised to produce dead gold for the person who pays for my researches.'

The mixture was ready ground now, a greyish powder with pinhead reddish-yellow grains in it. He took the mortar from her and poured the powder with great care on to a slab of polished stone, which he then pushed on to the embers. His face was tense, his lips moving. He beckoned to Bonadea to come closer and she went so close she could feel the heat fierce on her face. With chalk, he drew a circle on the floor, all round them and up over the hearth, fixing the chalk into a pair of tongs and completing the circle across the sooty wall.

The powder slowly blackened and began to reek. Herr Turiam whispered. When he stopped to draw breath, they could hear a faint singing note. Bonadea thought she had heard it before somewhere, in a storm perhaps, or no, it reminded her more of light from thick clouds; she began to feel dizzy ... Herr Turiam's voice thundered between the cellar walls, the tone changing to a whine and dying away again.

Annoyed and frightened, Bonadea thought: 'I'm fainting.' She bent forward and put her head between her knees, knowing that you could cure fainting fits like that.

When her head had cleared and she looked up, the powder was nothing but a black and sticky dollop on the stone slab. With a palette knife, Herr Turiam scraped it off and put it into a glass crucible, which he then filled with water and placed on a three-legged stand. Then he shovelled more charcoal on to the fire. 'Are you tired?' he said. 'Not? Good. The first step was successful.'

The water in the crucible gradually filled with pearls, then darkened when the paste dissolved. The steam rising from it alternated between blue and green. Herr Turiam held his hand in it. It smelt nasty.

Then faintly, a long way away, they heard a voice, unwilling, indistinct and harsh. Herr Turiam mumbled excited words, the same ones over and over again ... the harsh voice died away into a snore.

'Not strong enough,' said Herr Turiam. His eyes were glowing and he was looking round jerkily. 'I should have used egg after all – no one can resist egg – not in conjunction with . . .'

'I can go and get one,' said Bonadea, hoping for an opportunity to *breathe* for a while up there in the kitchen, but before she had time to do more than get up, he had pressed her down again.

'Don't go outside the circle,' he said roughly. He opened the door in the tower-like stove and with an asbestos glove on his hand, took out the fire-vulture's egg.

'But we were going to hatch it out!' cried Bonadea, but he took no notice of her. He let it glide down into the crucible. A thunderous roar rolled round them – the whole house must be shaking, she thought, the whole town. Flames shot out, but through the roaring sound, she could hear Herr Turiam's voice, triumphant now, and the other voice, the answering voice from far away, complaining shrilly. Bonadea could not catch any of the words, but the meaning of what was said sank into her all the same. The voice from nowhere said: 'You've no right to know the word, you haven't gone far enough yet. Knowledge that is not preceded by experience is evil . . . I won't tell you.'

'You're to tell me the word,' said Herr Turiam. 'Tell me. I am the stronger. I command you . . .'

Bonadea was beset with shudders from her hair right down to her toes, and she clasped her hands together. She had heard such a voice before, a lament just like that, when a man had been run over by his own cart on Heaven Hill. He had tried to keep silent, but had been unable to. Herr Turiam's hand in the cloud of steam trembled. It was red and wet, but he kept it there and went on mumbling.

Then he leant forward in extreme excitement. The voice was speaking words that stayed hanging in the air, echoing, trembling between the walls – there was a clicking in the fireproof glass of the crucible. Herr Turiam raised his voice, raised it violently – and at that moment the crucible cracked and hissing steam billowed out. Bonadea hurled herself to one side.

Herr Turiam grabbed her by the back of the 'wolf' so that she would not step over the chalk circle line, holding her firmly until the steam evaporated. The egg had totally vanished.

Crestfallen, Bonadea remembered how she had thought of feeding the little vulture chick, with mice perhaps, and Cacklehilda would have been its foster-mother.

Herr Turiam wiped all the chalk away with a rag. 'There we are, then,' he said, going over to a window. He opened it and then opened the door to the cellar passage, all his movements exhausted and uncertain.

His papers rustled in the night wind and midges came whining in. Bonadea pressed her nose deep into the good smell of fish and tar of the 'wolf', and her voice muffled by the wool, she said: 'I don't want to be part of it any more now. It was all so horrible, all that.'

She had thought he would be angry and terrible, and she clenched her fists and her teeth against him. But he didn't appear to have heard what she had said. He was standing over by the window, the locks of hair fluttering round his old face. He was breathing deeply and wiping the sweat off his forehead with one sleeve. 'We managed it,' he said. 'The risk is always great when you use poisonous substances. And if I hadn't had an egg handy, it would have all been to no avail, anyhow. It was thanks to you it succeeded.'

Bonadea blinked.

He smiled slightly at her, his face indescribably furrowed and ravaged, but reflecting the glow from the embers. 'Did you hear what he said?'

'No . . . not so that I understood.'

'But I did,' he said, lowering his eyelids. 'I heard the word. Short cut or no short cut, I possess the word now, and the time is near – next time the moon wanes will be the crucial and ultimate test. Then the sun runs in the sign of the Lion, and the mutual position of the planets is favourable. I found out the practical details long ago.'

Bonadea hunched up inside the 'wolf', thinking that when she had agreed to become a member of this peculiar household, she had clearly known nothing about anything. But now she thought she had a certain responsibility towards Herr Turiam and could not withdraw just like that. There were many days until the moon waned.

She went to bed, totally exhausted. After she had been asleep for a while, she had a nightmare. It was obscure and colourless, but full of heavy thumping, and just when she could no longer stand it, she heard a joyful, strong voice singing out there on the other side of the wall, and it was singing the old dancing song *Thief, thief, you shall be called, because you stole my little friend.* But the continuation was not the usual *But I have the only answer, because I'll get another* and instead ran *But I have the only answer, because I'll get her back.*

The voice sang the verse over and over again. She recognized it: Black Sea Sailor, and it rang in her ears long after she had woken up.

SEVEN
The Gold

The next day was cloudy. When Bonadea came yawning and heavy-headed into the kitchen, the housekeeper placed food in front of her, coffee, too, and a bun loaf, quite unasked. The food was good, a beef stew. The housekeeper took a cup of coffee and sat down at the table opposite her.

'How did it go last night?' she asked abruptly.

'Quite well, Herr Turiam said,' said Bonadea cautiously.

'Oh, yes, as long as he escapes with his life, all's always well. He staggers out of the ruins, blood-stained and lamed, and dizzy in the head, and says all's *well*. I've never known a man flourish so on adversity – as if one disappointment on top of another were simply sweet milk. I heard the bang all right. But I want to know – did you see anything?'

'Nothing special – steam and smoke.'

'Uhuh,' said the housekeeper, relaxing a little, twisting her gold rings round in her ears. 'Have some more food. You might think I was a bad cook, you eat so little. I only ask because no one can stand absolutely anything for ever, and he stretches himself so far, and risks everything he has, the silly old man. I know one of those meddlers, an ambitious *adept*, or whatever fine name it is they use, another demon just like Turiam –

Horst his name is – who did the Eckhartshausen experiment. Eckhartshausen himself was almost poisoned, in fact, but Horst, he called up a phantom and then had to face it day and night for years and years afterwards. It was less clear in the daylight, of course. But if he happened to look at anything dark – a shadow or a black door – then it was indeed revealed.'

In all her time at Gripander House, Bonadea had never heard the housekeeper say so much, and there was suddenly something familiar about her way of speaking.

'Have some more,' she said. 'While there still is some. It's not paid for, like everything else in this house.'

'How did you come to be here in Tulavall of all places?' said Bonadea. She had had enough to eat now, and without greed, dipped her slice of bunloaf into her coffee.

The housekeeper snorted. 'I was born here. In Crowfield. There was eight of us before mamma died. Then pappa took us all and my uncle's lot to America. Eleven cousins we were altogether. Well, it went well and it didn't – made a change for us, anyhow.'

She clamped her mouth shut but then opened it again to say: 'My family still live up at Crowfield, but I can't be bothered to seek them out, with *that* round my neck.' She nodded in towards the house.

After another pause, she said with a crooked smile: 'I'm not even asking you to keep quiet about this, because now I know you don't gossip.'

For several days on end, Jakem had been doing a strange job, measuring with a plummet and a spirit level, boring holes through floors and ceilings. When Bonadea went down to the cellar the evening the moon was on the wane, Herr Turiam was standing with his head back, peering straight up into the sky. He shouted, and up on the metal roof of Gripander House, Jakem answered with a hoarse bellow.

Then Herr Turiam arranged several stands, nailed together with small strips of wood on his directions by Jakem, in a circle beneath the hole. Then he hung small mirrors on them, so that some of them reflected the sky, and others reflected the reflection of the sky – he adjusted them for a long time before he was satisfied. Bonadea sat watching in a corner.

'What's that going to be?' she said.

Herr Turiam did not always answer her questions, but this time he chuckled silently and said: 'We're going to catch a star tonight.'

The housekeeper came hurrying in, shut the door behind her and leant back against it. 'He's here again,' she said in a subdued voice. 'I said you were busy. But he's angry and insisted.'

Herr Turiam said in annoyance: 'I haven't time for him now.'

'He's coming along the passage. I can hear him,' said the housekeeper in a low voice. 'Off you go,' she said to Bonadea, pointing towards the hatch up in the wall. 'Hide up there for the time being. No need to make things more complicated than we have to,' she said to Herr Turiam, who nodded. Bonadea flew up the wobbly ladder. She opened the hatch door, tumbled through it and pushed it shut behind her.

She was in a room she had never been in before. It was very bright after the half-light of the cellar. The window was high up and when she stood on tiptoe, she could see across the square. There were rows of unpainted shelves along the walls, all full of glass bottles, jars and vessels – all dusty and most of them empty – but they reflected the light from a cloud coloured by the setting sun. There seemed to be fire in them, smouldering firelight and perilous forces that might at any moment burst the bottles apart – at the sound of a word, perhaps, or perhaps a strong feeling alone would be enough to release them.

She could hear voices from down in the cellar. Herr Turiam said: 'I've nothing new to tell you now. Tomorrow . . .'

'Tomorrow! You've said that every day ever since you came,' replied Herr Klingkors. Bonadea recognized his voice, although it sounded much colder and harsher and more unpleasant than when he came to see them or spoke to people in the streets or the square.

'I give you my word of honour that . . .'

Herr Klingkors interrupted again: 'What do I care about your honour? It's gold I want – the gold you promised me – and I need it now. You've no idea what risks I'm taking, what sacrifices I've made to acquire your material – more and more and more for your insatiable ovens. And all you've given me in return has been promises. Now I'm telling you – I've come to the end.'

His voice was shaking, as if from fear or excitement. He coughed. Or perhaps it had been just the shaking of a cough? He went on: 'I cannot guarantee your safety for ever. I have used my confidential position to your advantage. But now the interests of the town are at stake . . .'

'Don't you come with all that! I've known you since we collected tadpoles in Surbrunn pool,' said the housekeeper. 'You don't seem to have changed much since then, although you've acquired a silver-topped cane and moustaches and wax to wax them with – and a fancy name, to boot! You're up to something no good, otherwise you wouldn't come crawling like a worm, and suddenly be in such an urgent hurry that you can scarcely stay inside your shoes. I wonder what kind of money it is you've provided us with, though you said it was yours. And I'll have you know, Herr Turiam has never promised you anything else but that he would do his best.'

Bonadea peered through the crack. Herr Klingkors was chewing on his moustache. Herr Turiam had turned his back on them and was rustling his papers in the corner.

'But . . .' said Herr Klingkors finally, his voice shrill and snarling. 'This is intolerable! We may well have known each other as children – that's a very long time ago. Herr Turiam,' he went on insistently. 'I have not come here to be insulted by your servant. You must understand that the situation is serious – something has happened that I do not wish to go into further in the presence of – hm – a third person, but believe me . . .'

Herr Turiam spoke from his desk, still with his back turned. 'Every person who attempts to seek into what for that person is new knowledge runs the risk of being confused by what is demanded of his mind and in particular his memory. I realize that you have forgotten the results I showed you when you were last here.'

Then he turned round. With a few steps, he was facing Herr Klingkors, looking straight at him. 'I can promise you the gold tonight. Come again at two o'clock.'

Neither of them said another word. Herr Klingkors put his hat on and backed away towards the door. The housekeeper went all the way out with him, just to make sure.

Bonadea took courage and came down. Herr Turiam called to Jakem and told him to put a soap-stone vessel on the fire and fill it with rain-water. They made their preparations as they had made their preparations innumerable times before, all through the summer. The nights were already dark now. One experiment had led to another in one long chain, just as when you made yoghourt, Bonadea thought, always taking a bit of the previous day's to use each day. But yoghourt was white, and the experiments were different every time. Sometimes they became nothing but black smoke, and mostly were as incomprehensible as the games of little children. But Herr Turiam said each time that now he knew a little more than before.

That night he knew enough to lure a star into his possession. With powerful words he had forced out of the dead, with the help of the position of the planets and the darkness of the moon, with substances so insignificant in appearance and as full of mighty powers as seeds that he threw into the stone cauldron, and with a hazel stick with which Bonadea had to stir counter-clockwise, they would have power over the star and would transform it.

'Will a whole star manage to get into that little cauldron?' Bonadea said.

He laughed silently, his eyes glittering: 'Yes, and the cauldron will be so heavy that no one will be able to move it. And it's contents will increase ... and improve ... for ever, or almost.'

The housekeeper came in with food on a tray, but he ate little.

In the mirrors, the patch of sky slowly changed colour, growing bluer and bluer.

Everything was ready. Jakem and the housekeeper had gone. Herr Turiam stood beneath the hole and peered. Then he stepped to one side. The star was as he had calculated, directly above the house, and showed in all the mirrors as gossamer white down. Bonadea was given the sign and began to stir the water. Then Herr Turiam started reciting his incantation.

Bonadea tried to make out what it was he was saying, but sometimes it only sounded like 'ooommanintemee ... omaninteme' and sometimes just like 'hersher hersh'.

For a long time nothing happened, except that the water in which the powerful substances were gradually dissolving began to simmer. Bonadea stirred and stirred, so that a hollow counter-clockwise whirlpool was formed. She thought she *saw* Herr Turiam's powerful obstinate will, his accumulated toil, rising like a column to an immeasurable height – but it was she, Bonadea, with her hazel stick, who was making it whirl, and it was the whirlpool's force that was to draw the star down out of the skies, a tornado in reverse, sucking it down into the cauldron.

Herr Turiam had said: 'You needn't be afraid as long as you stir counter-clockwise. It won't splash or burn. It'll slide quite quietly, lower and lower, until it is extinguished and becomes gold.'

She stirred, and it was like winding wool. At every turn, the star came closer, but it was an immeasurable distance to wind in.

Gradually the mirrors began to glow more and more brightly. Bonadea closed her eyes and counted to a hundred and then looked up again. Yes, silver sparks were streaming out of the mirrors and joining in the air into a swirling globe. Herr Turiam raised his voice.

There was an eternity of waiting, but then suddenly the star was there in the room itself, between the floor and the ceiling – a globe of white mist out of which shafts were darting, as thick and close as hairs of a fur, without ceasing. Herr Turiam gabbled faster. The star glided closer to Bonadea, trembling nearer and nearer to the upward-curling vapours.

Bonadea bit her lip, the hazel stick now going round and round more or less on its own, and yet still heavy to move. Her body was numb and stiff, and yet it was shaking, and her throat was aching. A star, what was a star? She had read in one of Herr Turiam's books that they were as large as the earth, as large as whole worlds. Some were just clouds of glowing gases, others cold, of stone and metal – it made no difference. 'In all of nature, there is nothing wholly without life.' And now all the life that existed in this particular star had taken shape in the living heavenly fire before her, and it was condemned to die.

When it had been forced down into the cauldron, its place in the sky would be empty, never again to show seamen the way across the oceans. But Herr Turiam would have his gold. The star was just about to touch the vapour.

Its brilliance had faded. Herr Turiam's voice was tense.

And then . . . Bonadea stirred clockwise.

It was heavy going making the hazel stick obey. She had to use all her strength, as if she were stopping a bolting horse, and the simmering water suddenly felt thick and heavy.

But the cellar was filled with light, not white, but as yellow as honey. And in the middle of the light glowed a figure rather like a salamander, but larger than any she had seen before. Also rather like an angel. It moved in glittering curves, and appeared to be transparent, as if created out of newly blossoming fire-leaves round a kernel of even stronger light. It was so beautiful and so terrible, and its expression of violent jubilant ecstasy was so overwhelming that the two human beings in the cellar felt all their bones weakening.

Then Bonadea felt how she, too, was swept up, as the star was released and rushed back up into the skies. She tried to resist and turn and grasp something, but there was nothing to grasp, and her body was not even with her, but had been left down on earth.

At first it was nothing but crackling haste, and out in the great darkness the stars were like sparks. At closer range, they resembled silver ornaments, shining and singing, great globes of light. Closer even, she could discern movements on their surfaces, flowers or bubbles or splashing foam, rushing falls, as if light were being poured out of wide vessels all over her.

She approached a light which was more brilliant than everything else, a light that swelled and flooded towards her. But every time she gasped and thought . . . now! now! — it will fill the whole world! – here is the centre of everything! – a broad belt round the perimeter loosened and swirled towards her. Now she was flying through a tunnel with walls consisting of alternating darkness and circles of light, bells ringing, or was it waves breaking? – not on to the shore, for there were no shores here, but towards her consciousness.

The torrents of light that washed over her and struck through her were laden with insight. She felt herself stretched taut, and almost broken. Now she knew and understood: she was in the universe and the earth was nothing but a distant speck.

'Yes,' she thought. 'I've known that, all the time, I've *known* it – but it is terrible and difficult and desolating to know. I can stand no more and I want to go home.' But she went on in a swinging rhythm like that of ships and waves, though there was nothing there but darkness and light, and she slid closer to a brilliant beating heart.

'I don't want to leave the earth now – not leave – the dandelions,' she thought. Her memory touched lightly on faces and hands, and her grief over everything she had already forgotten pained her.

Then she heard her name being called.

'What happened? What happened?' someone was shouting.

And Bonadea blinked. She was back in the cellar, but it seemed to be filled with dark water. The fire in the hearth was also dark, dark red. She rubbed her eyes.

The housekeeper came rushing across the floor, tripping over a stool and throwing herself down on her knees. Bonadea had the impression that she had been through this before, she didn't know where, but it was like the verse:

Then the great river ceased
that before had run so free
and the brown-haired deer
forgot where he should flee

Then she made out Herr Turiam lying on the floor. The housekeeper had his head cradled in her arms. 'Bonadea!' she cried. 'Fetch some water.'

Bonadea could not manage an answer, but she got up and leant against the wall. Then she stumbled her way across to the water-tub over by the door and back again with a scoopful she kept spilling. 'Tell me what happened!' cried the housekeeper.

Herr Turiam moved, then took a few sips of water. 'It broke loose,' he said hoarsely. As he spoke, his voice grew clearer. 'It broke loose, I don't know why . . . it shouldn't have been able to . . . at the last moment. Yes, at the very end.' He hauled himself laboriously to his feet.

Then he laughed as if in wonder. 'Is this how it is to end?' he said. 'One thinks of so many possibilities, but *never* can one calculate exactly how it will go.'

'Don't talk like that,' said the housekeeper. 'So long as you escape with your life, then all is well. You're just a bit dizzy in the head. I'll get you a drop of spirits, or would you rather have coffee?'

But he laughed again, quite slowly, bubbling in his throat like a pigeon. 'I have reached what I have sought all my days. The arcanum of heavenly fire. And it's so simple, one can only laugh with relief. But it is just *light* throughout. One cannot explain. One cannot say anything in words. Come here, Gunna, where are you? I can't see you.'

She stared straight into his eyes, then covered her face with her hands and burst into tears. Between her sobs, she managed to say something about not failing as long as one has not given up.

'But I haven't failed,' he said patiently. 'On the contrary.'

'I knew,' said the housekeeper, and her speech struggled with her tears so that she slurred and stammered her words, 'that a person could not tolerate just anything, and I probably knew he would go mad sooner or later, but it's terrible, terrible . . .'

'It's strange,' he said, as before. 'As long as I endeavoured blindly, you stood by me against the rest of the world. And all the misery I brought on your head, and now that my search is at an end, you want to betray me and no longer believe my word.' As if searching, his eyes flickered round until they came to rest on Bonadea.

The housekeeper looked at him, blinked quickly and swallowed. Then she said: 'I'm not betraying you. I'll stick to you all right. You must forgive me for being a bit upset by all this . . . and we've got that Klingkors coming in an hour.'

'Let him come. He is of no significance,' said Herr Turiam, smiling into the air as if he could still see the star in front of him.

The housekeeper bit her lip, then spoke quickly with pauses in between to give her time to think. 'He hasn't the kind of head that means he can understand what you're talking about. We must show ourselves to be stronger than he is. He's said he doesn't want your honour, so we can do what we like with that. But he's been promised gold, and he shall have gold so that it sets his teeth on edge. Better that he curses us than laughs at us – or pities us.'

As speedily as the star had disappeared, all things beautiful in the world vanished, leaving you blinded. And the river flowed away, away. And the deer leapt, far, far away. And that was the agony of night and sorrow. But the stars existed, just like strength and sweetness and glory. That always had to be remembered, though they were mostly so distant to be scarcely visible, and burnt you and changed you the moment they were close. Bonadea was so absorbed in her efforts to remember, that she hardly noticed what was going on around her. Jakem and the housekeeper were rummaging about. They had shovelled up all the embers left in the tower-oven and put pieces of charcoal on. Jakem was working the bellows and the housekeeper was watching something she had placed in a crucible.

Then she touched Bonadea on the shoulder and Bonadea leapt up. 'Move aside.' She had taken out the crucible and was holding it in some tongs – it was a very battered crucible, more like a small hollowed-out brick with crumbling edges. The hollow was lined with borax that had melted into gruel and the gruel was floating like a shimmering yellow blob of butter. The housekeeper knocked the blob out on to the floor. Bonadea noticed that she no longer had her rings in her ears.

'We'll have to be content with inner honour and leave with it,' muttered the housekeeper. 'And leave at once.' She flung the crucible away, far in amongst the charcoal and ash.

Jakem had opened the old iron door behind the fireplace and

was hacking away with a crowbar at the earthen floor, levering up great chunks.

'Klingkors, that turncoat, he's in no danger. He's always been a big-mouth, but if anyone can turn in midair and come down the right way again, then he can. Bonadea, I really meant to give that dress of yours a wash. Goodbye to you now. If you stay in this house until sunrise, then you'll be free of us. Jakem!' She spoke to him in that foreign language and then continued after he had put the crowbar aside and trudged out. 'He'll have to make his own way. But we reckon to meet him in Riga – or at Trinkenstein Castle – or in Mithonggatka.'

Bonadea swallowed and swallowed and managed to get out a whisper: 'What shall I say to Herr Klingkors?'

'You're not to say anything to him. He doesn't know you're here. You can hide anywhere you like, and as soon as day breaks, you can go. But *him*, Turiam, has released such powerful forces tonight, one living soul must be here to enchain them – simply the presence of warmth – that's what he used to say. Well, he probably would have explained it to you much better than I can, and he would also have released you from service in a better way and given you other wages than a pair of shoes. But he'll probably get better as long as he gets some rest,' she concluded anxiously.

She put her arm round Herr Turiam and hauled him to his feet. He was looking straight ahead. His face was calm and the air round him was still, not trembling as it had done earlier. 'Goodbye, Bonadea,' the housekeeper said once again over her shoulder.

Bonadea was left alone. She could see more clearly now. The gold patch shone faintly on the uneven floor. In the cauldron, the water was swirling clockwise and she thought sluggishly that perhaps it would have to turn as many revolutions that way as it had earlier the other way.

EIGHT
The Night

She had promised to watch and wait, and she did so up in her room. The wind had risen now, a fresh wet wind, and the house was full of sounds, cracklings and creakings all round her, the metal roof rumbling. The trees in the garden and in West Wood beat against each other and now and again shook themselves, opening their branches like outspread arms. When she leant out of the window, she could see her star.

It had moved a little and would move another span before daybreak. She was pleased to see it and to know it was secure – it would be there on course long after she and Herr Turiam and the housekeeper and all the people whose hearts had been scorched and fingers burnt were dead. And seamen would be able to navigate by it.

She looked at it and was pleased; yes, she was pleased, but at the same time she felt strangely tense and gloomy, rather like a lump of raw metal that had been violently heated up experimentally and then discarded. She seemed to have lost all the warmth she had ever possessed, causing her heart to shrink to the size of a mouse's ear; and it was painful.

She stood by the window for a long time, listening to the wind tugging and the waves roaring over there on the shore.

The sky grew paler and filled with clouds. The night lightened.

In the grey shadowless half-light, she saw something moving on the opposite side of the square. It was an animal, rather like a small fox or a cat with a bushy tail. It was grey. It nosed its way out of Water Sprite Lane, sniffed the air and began to run up across the square, heading straight for Gripander House, moving lithely. Directly beneath Bonadea's window, it stopped and looked up and she met its eyes.

That very moment, fear and terror shot through her in a scalding wave; she was so frightened that it hurt right out to her finger-tips, because the eyes in that animal face were human eyes, and they were evil. The animal stared straight into her eyes, then lowered its head and slithered in through a hole in the stone foundations of the house.

And the house, that had stood there empty, rocking and rumbling in the wind, was now filled with a terrifying force, a threat oozing and thrusting its way through the walls. 'Hush,' she said to herself, stiff-leggedly hobbling over to the door and locking it. 'Keep your heart burning like a sun,' she said to herself, thumping her fist on her chest. But her heart pecked unevenly and faintly back in reply, and if it were burning, then it was certainly with a very feeble flame. She sat down on the edge of the bed and thought aloud: 'Don't be frightened. There's nothing to be frightened of . . . as long as you're not afraid.' She tried to impress it deeply upon her mind and at the same time think about the dawn to come. But she found it hard work when she was in reality absorbed in listening and listening and keeping herself perfectly still, so that no one should know where she was – that she even *existed* – no earthly visitor, anyhow.

Then she heard the dull sound of footsteps up on the roof, immediately above her head. She had often heard gulls pattering about up there in the early mornings. They made such a noise on the sheet-metal plates that they might well have been mistaken for large men. But it was far too early for gulls now, and it *was* a man. He leapt down on to her balcony and stood up, dark against the grey sky. She recognized him from his movements. It was Black Sea Sailor.

He opened the balcony door and crossed the floor in two strides, then fell to his knees by the bed and flung his arms round her stiff tense body. He was bony and sinewy and warm and he was breathing heavily. She let her head sink down against his shoulder and felt his beard on her cheek. 'Have you been running?' she said.

The earth turned and the night blew away. He held her hand and now all was well. She began to tell him what had happened since the last time, but the complications were over and she had nothing to complain about, not even the housekeeper's sharp fingers. 'But how do you know?' she said. 'How do you know how to come and rescue me, always just in time? Do you feel it in your bones?'

He laughed a little. 'Yes, I probably do.'

'But if you go further away, then you won't be in time, even if you do feel it in your bones – and me doing all kinds of things all the time . . .' She felt the tears rising and tried to swallow them.

He laughed and stroked her face with the whole of his hand. 'I'll be on time, little one. Even if it's from the end of the earth. Don't believe anything else, little *tippa*.'

He told her he had seen the housekeeper and Herr Turiam far out at sea – they were standing upright, like an invisible craft obeying neither wind nor waves – heading westwards at great speed. Herr Turiam was standing on the housekeeper's feet and she had her arms around him.

Bonadea must have slept for a while, because she woke when he put her down on the floor and said: 'Now we can go.' The golden cockerel on the Town Hall tower was glowing, then turned dull as the sky clouded over.

She remembered to take the bark-boats off the window-sill, as well as the red shoes that were the only wages she had earned. 'Ssh,' said Black Sea Sailor on the stairs, 'I can hear something . . .'

It was voices and doors and stamping footsteps. 'It must be Klingkors,' whispered Bonadea. 'But he was going to come at two o'clock, and I didn't hear him. Unless *that* was him, of course. And just imagine, I'd thought of going to get myself a sandwich before I went!'

'He may have come and gone again, and just sounded like the wind, and now he's come back again with witnesses,' Black Sea Sailor whispered back. 'But you can have a sandwich all the same.'

They waited until the noisy company had descended the cellar steps, then crept out into the kitchen where Bonadea took bread and butter and cold potatoes. 'Aren't you going to have any?' she asked Black Sea Sailor, and he replied: 'Not just yet.'

They could see the round head of Brasse the policeman through the kitchen window and hear the dignified creaking of his boots. 'We'll take the front way, shall we?' said Black Sea Sailor, and Bonadea nodded, her mouth full. They slipped out into the pantry just as the cellar door opened, and then into the corridor, and the hall, and the porch, where it was an easy task to open the front door. Bonadea locked it again from the outside and threw the key through the letter-box. 'There we are!' she said radiantly.

'Wait a moment,' said Black Sea Sailor, going over to the corner. A subdued and angry argument could be heard from down in the work-cellar. The windows inside the iron grids had been opened and occasional voices could be heard above the others.

'Fraudulently ... fled, yes ... but is there any *evidence* the flight was a conspiracy involving anyone else or any of the town worthies?'

Herr Klingkors growled agitatedly in reply: 'I assure you I'm just as upset and disturbed as you are – yes, even more so, as I've invested such large sums in the enterprise. I had the good of the town at heart. A whole new industry. As valuable as any natural gold-mine. Work for hundreds of people ... flourishing ... progressive ... contacts abroad ...'

'Is there any evidence that he did in fact succeed in making gold?'

'The evidence lies here on the floor – a spilt piece they didn't even bother with.'

Then the voices all ran into each other again. 'Yes, we're grateful to you, Herr Klingkors, for discovering the escape in time. Shouldn't we summon the mayor all the same? Now that telegrams have been sent out and all the ports closed ... but they can't have got far with such a heavy load, can they? You can see how they dug the gold out of the floor where they had hidden it.'

The wind was full of scents, powerful, sharp and fresh; scents of birch leaves and damp earth and salt from the sea. 'Where shall we go now?' said Bonadea, and the joy of being allowed to come and go as she pleased, however and whenever she wished, rushed through her and lifted her from the ground in leap after leap. She ran across the square, her arms flailing.

From under the grass of West Wood, dew on its nose, a small hedgehog came towards her, twisting and turning in several directions in that way hedgehogs do. It raised its snout and its black eyes glittered at Bonadea, as if laughing at her. Then it ran off and vanished between the iron railings into Gripander House garden.

Wide-eyed, Bonadea watched it go, then said: 'Can Klockarback-Fia turn herself into a hedgehog?'

'It seems so, doesn't it?' said Black Sea Sailor.

'Then I've heard her rustling about several times. So I haven't been as alone as I thought.'

'One hardly ever is. Come, we're going to Rummelstrand today. Old Fridburg usually ties up at the middle quay.'

In the middle of the bridge, in the roaring wind, he took her hand in his and stopped. When she turned towards him, he stepped back a step, for a moment holding her at arm's length, and he smiled a smile in which a hundred secrets were dancing, in which there was tenderness, too, as well as melancholy. 'Bonadea,' he said. 'Go up to Rummelbacken's big rock, climb up on to it and wait until you see the *Fina* coming in. Then you can walk down to the middle quay and meet me there.'

'But you can't go now!' she cried. 'You've only just come!'

He said: 'I'll be on my way to you as straight as the gull flies,' and the next moment he was gone. She was left standing there with her arms outstretched and her hands empty in the air.

The wind swept her hair away from her face and filled her worn red-checked skirt. Gulls soared above her, swooped down and rose again. After only a little while, her dismay had vanished and happiness and expectation filled and elevated her – she laughed and rushed as fast as she could across the bridge and up on to Rummelbacken, clambering up the slope where the pine trees waggled their skirts as if dancing on the spot. She ran along the fence round the new cemetery and flew on up to the big rock, then up on to the top of it.

There she stood. A great landscape of huge clouds was rolling above the sea – white, silvery and stormy blue. Far away to the south-east, as gossamer-like as a mirage, she could just discern a boat heading inland. To the west, the whole island world had vanished into grey rain, and a rainbow arched like a waterfall down into the brilliantly shining streaky water.